BLIMP!

Photography by
GEORGE HALL
and
BARON WOLMAN
Text by
GEORGE LARSON
Design by
NEIL SHAKERY

VNR VAN NOSTRAND REINHOLD COMPANY
New York Cincinnati Toronto London Melbourne

With heartfelt thanks to
the pilots and crews of the airships
America, Columbia, Mayflower, Enterprise,
and *Europa,* we dedicate this book to
those who truly sail the skies.

Library of Congress Catalog Card Number 81-218
ISBN 0-442-29608-8

Printed in the United States of America.

Published by Van Nostrand Reinhold Company
135 West 50th Street
New York, NY 10020

Van Nostrand Reinhold Limited
1410 Birchmount Road
Scarborough, Ontario M1P 2E7, Canada

Van Nostrand Reinhold Australia Pty. Ltd.
17 Queen Street
Mitcham, Victoria 3132, Australia

Van Nostrand Reinhold Company Limited
Molly Millars Lane
Wokingham, Berkshire, England

Photo credits:
Page 29, Wide World.
Pages 24, 25, 42, 43, History of Aviation
Collection, University of Texas at Dallas.

16 15 14 13 12 11 10 9 8 7 6 5 4 3 2 1

Library of Congress Cataloging in Publication Data

Main entry under title:

Blimp!

Includes index.
1. Air-ships. I. Hall, George (George N.)
II. Wolman, Baron. III. Larson, George C.
IV. Shakery, Neil.
TL656.2.B5 629.133'27 81-218
ISBN 0-442-29608-8 AACR2

CONTENTS

Goodyear's blimps are the airships with which the world is most familiar. No other operator has as much experience as Goodyear with its fleet of blimps, which have roamed the U.S. and Europe for years.

This book was begun in 1972, when George Hall, a photographer, was assigned to shoot a story for a magazine. Although that assignment had nothing to do with blimps, it took Hall to an area where the *Mayflower*, one of Goodyear's original public relations airships, was operating. Hall got lucky and snapped up a ride on the blimp, and that experience started a kind of love affair that lasted for four years. Hall photographed blimps in the daytime and at night, blimps flying, blimps in repose, the blimp's-eye view of the world. Much of the material ended up illustrating some spectacular calendars for Goodyear, but the rest was saved for a book. Nobody was sure exactly what kind of book it would be, only that there would be plenty of blimp in it.

Despite many efforts to find a backer for his book idea, Hall got no takers until he met Baron Wolman, another photographer whom he immediately infected with the blimp photo-bug. Now both Wolman and Hall were filling their closets with blimp photos. Wolman, however, had his own publishing company, Squarebooks, and he decided to undertake the project. That first Squarebooks edition of *The Blimp Book* was produced by the same team of Hall, Larson, Wolman, and Shakery that brings you the present volume; its graphics and writing won several awards for excellence.

When Baron Wolman went looking for investors willing to underwrite the project, he found his chief ally in Michael Wittman, a former public relations staffer with one of the Goodyear airships now in New York City, once again on duty with the fleet. Wittman asked Calvin Bentsen and Vannie Cook, Jr., to give at the office, and both did so, generously. Without the quiet confidence and financial support of those two investors, the first edition of this book would never have gotten off the ground—if you'll forgive us the phrase.

Goodyear was unhesitatingly generous with its resources as well. Robert Lane deserves the ultimate credit for keeping the blimps flying for so many years when others might have allowed the public relations program to be dropped. Tom Allison and Tom Riley of Goodyear contributed information from the very recesses of the company's archives.

During the time we have been involved with this book, we have worked with innumerable crew members, and in every case, they have opened doors of knowledge to us and shared their hospitality, often beyond the call of duty.

Now you are about to meet Son of *Blimp Book*. This revised and expanded edition has been encouraged by some extraordinary people at Van Nostrand Reinhold: Richard Pohanish and Barbara Ravage, who generously provided inspiration and direction to this edition.

For research assistance and photographic reinforcement, we turned to G. Edward Rice, curator of the History of Aviation Collection at the University of Texas at Dallas. At this collection resides the treasure of the papers of airship pioneer Charles Rosendahl, his complete personal library of blimp and airship memorabilia, comprising original papers, invaluable data, and photographs, many of them heretofore unpublished. Rice and his staff and friends of the collection gave of their time and energies as though this project were their own. We are in their debt.

Bill Coleman and Karl Stefan of U.S. Airships found the time amid the organizational pains of a brand-new company to talk about their past and their future.

Dr. Jack R. Hunt is the president of Embry-Riddle Aeronautical University and has plenty to fill his day. Still, he found the time to talk about some of the U.S. Navy's experience with airships, and in that devotion to history he is typical of lighter-than-air fliers. In all other respects, Hunt is anything but a typical man; if he is not careful, someone will attach a plaque to him and have him declared a national treasure.

Paul J. Siemer of Fleishman-Hillard, St. Louis, as well as Jim Ahern of World Balloon Corporation in Albuquerque, provided the information about the Anheuser-Busch blimps.

Finally, Dale E. Williams and Jean M. Vocar of Goodyear Aerospace willingly devoted time away from their tasks at hand to talk about the future of airships and, in particular, the specific programs within their company. From that, we were able to make critical judgments in an area that is too often characterized by hype and pie-in-the-sky.

Those of us who labored on the original *Blimp Book* present this new, updated version in the knowledge that, even as we write, things are changing for airships as fast as they have ever changed before. We sense that there will be much more to write about in the years to come.

GEORGE LARSON

1

BEHOLD THE BLIMP!

The perfect symmetry of a blimp—here, the *Columbia*—is the essence of aerodynamics. Its beauty and purity of form can totally captivate any onlooker.

Of all the flying machines devised by man, only airships are truly at home in the skies. Being the only airborne vehicles that are both buoyant and controllable in the air, blimps often seem touched by a spirit that is not of this world. Heavier-than-air craft such as airplanes and helicopters are all commotion and bluster compared with the serenity of a blimp. Even from a great distance, the sight of a blimp in flight can transfix the senses and grip the imagination.

The blimp's very nature is contradictory: it is huge, yet insubstantial; it suggests the shape of speed, yet it trundles through the air like a skyborne hippo. Its shiny metallic envelope, seemingly a polished, monomorphic dart, is really a thin membrane, an undulating bladder swollen by the restless gases within. Beneath this great bag, like a remora on a shark, hangs the car. It dangles like an afterthought, yet it is the blimp's sole cargo. At the helm, a flyspeck of a human lends it intelligence.

The blimp's singular talent—its ability to hover without motion, utterly ignoring gravity—is an infinite resource. A blimp provides the flight that we ordinarily experience only in dreams: an effortless floating just above the treetops. As it noses to earth here and there like some mammoth bottom-feeder, it conveys an eternal patience. So out of step are its rhythms with our customary bustle that a blimp sometimes seems the product of an alien intelligence. Its size, shape, and majesty lend it the aura of a profound and mysterious purpose as it overlooks the aimless haste below.

These airships have been put to work at jobs ranging from combat to pure pleasure. The majority of the fleet flying today exists solely to make people happy, and few other machines so successfully achieve their aim. But a blimp evokes more than mere pleasure. This great tumid vessel has a unique allure that can elicit the wildest affection. Fall under its spell, and you may find yourself wishing somehow to embrace it.

It has its moods. A blimp conveys a gentle humor tinged with melancholy as it wanders like some gray, eternal ghost. But then it rises above the gloom at dusk to glow in the sun's fire. At night, the blimp looms in opaque skies, like an unseen phantom bearing all our fears. It beckons to the most innocent of children and the most cynical of grownups, promising in its shadow relief from care and trouble.

A blimp is pure fun, devoid of mischief. Although it may be an anachronism playing out its glory, its role will endure so long as the riddle of its allure remains unanswered. Its future must be measured not by the life expectancy of its moving parts but by the need simply to have it around—and that may last forever. Nobody doesn't love a blimp.

As a serious instrument of transportation, the blimp has been almost forgotten. The zeppelin, the great rigid airship of the 1920's and 1930's, was the only lighter-than-air craft to succeed as a transport, but it was merely an interim measure until the airplane could leap the oceans. The zeppelin was the ultimate expression of airship design. It was, however, as different from the blimp as a skyscraper is from a circus tent. The shape and structure of the rigid airship were defined by the metal lattice frame within it and the covering of fabric around it, whereas the nonrigid blimp owes its form only to the shape of the envelope and the pressure of the gas within it.

The principle upon which all lighter-than-air craft operate is as valid today as it was in their heyday. Whereas all heavier-than-air craft need forward motion to produce the lift necessary to keep them in the air, the blimp—or any dirigible, for that matter—does not. Blimps derive lift from natural buoyancy: a light gas (in this case, helium) contained within a bag displaces an equal volume of a heavier gas (the atmosphere) and produces lift. Although the net gain will vary with the differences in density between the helium and the atmosphere surrounding the bag, under ordinary conditions of air pressure and temperature a blimp will float with enough lift left over to carry a crew, engines, the fuel to run them, and maybe even a television camera. Best of all, this lift capacity can be put to work without using a drop of fuel.

An airplane in flight loses some of its driving energy to the induced drag resulting whenever its wings generate lift. A blimp, on the other hand, can use almost all of its motive power in simple forward or reverse motion. (Yes, blimps can back up.) A very small fraction of the blimp's motion may go into producing "dynamic lift," similar to that produced by an airplane's wing. But a blimp's ability to remain aloft without consuming very much energy makes it remarkably fuel-efficient—a fact that has led to recurring flurries of interest in the art of airship design and construction.

Airships are buoyed by helium, which carries aloft their entire dead weight. Their engines therefore need only provide forward motion, making airships exceptionally efficient.

A modern blimp can operate for a week on the amount of fuel a jumbo jet uses taxiing from the terminal to the runway. In March 1957, a U.S. Navy blimp called the *Snowbird* set an endurance record that still stands: the *Snowbird* flew for eleven days and 9,000 miles without refueling. The gigantic *Hindenburg* regularly crossed the Atlantic on about five hundred dollars' worth of diesel fuel at prices current then. But lighter-than-air craft have a maximum speed that is far less than a jet airplane's. Although that maximum speed has been revised upward over the years (currently, it is estimated to be about 120 miles per hour), airplanes will always be the faster machines. You can't have everything.

Blimps are the only controllable lighter-than-air craft flying today. Free balloons are lighter than air, too, but they have no rudder and must depend upon the air currents at various altitudes to get them where they are going. And no free balloon ever beat a course *into* the wind the way a blimp can.

The blimp is only one of three possible dirigible designs. The word *dirigible* (from the Latin *dirigere*, "to direct") defines all airships that are engine-driven and steerable. All airships are dirigibles and all dirigibles are airships.

Another dirigible design is the rigid airship, also called a zeppelin. A blimp cannot be a zeppelin, for a blimp is nonrigid. No rigid airships operate today, though a new company called Airships International wants to build a modern blimp with an all-metal skin made rigid by its "monocoque" construction, a method of building something so that its skin gives it strength—like an eggshell or a rolled-up piece of paper.

The third type of dirigible, the semirigid airship, operated a long time ago, but it too has passed from the scene. The semirigid airship was so named because it had a frame that ran the length of the envelope along the bottom. This keel was the only rigid structure on the airship. The rest of the hull consisted of a nonrigid envelope attached to the keel that took shape only as it filled with buoyant gas.

On a true blimp, the only rigid structures are the nose battens, the gondola, or car, and the control surfaces at the tail. The car hangs from a system of cables anchored to the top of the envelope. The control surfaces' bases are anchored to the envelope, and a system of structural wires similar to those used on biplanes aligns the surfaces properly.

The blimps flying today are not very large as blimps go. The U.S. Navy once operated a nonrigid airship called the ZPG-3W that was ten times the size of today's blimps. The volume of the *Hindenburg*'s hull was almost thirty times as great.

The origin of the word *blimp* has been the source of interminable argument. The idea that *blimp* was the contracted name of a British craft called a "balloon, type B, limp," was discounted following the discovery that no such craft ever existed. The Goodyear company, after considerable research, has determined that we owe the name to A. D. Cunningham and his playful thumb.

It is said that Cunningham, the commanding officer of a British air station at Capel, was conducting an inspection tour in 1915 and happened to snap his thumb against the fabric envelope of the SS-12, a nonrigid airship stationed there. The story goes that Commander Cunningham felt compelled, for reasons that are obscure, to imitate the sound his thumb had just made.

"Blimp!" said Cunningham.

So *blimp* it is.

Goodyear Tire & Rubber Company of Akron, Ohio, maintains and operates the only major fleet of commercial blimps. Other independent operators have come and gone, and new operations are being formed, but it is safe to say that it will be years before any new fleet acquires the experience of Goodyear's. Goodyear processes the envelopes from its own rubberized fabric: thus, it is a company ideally suited to operating its own fleet of blimps. But the company keeps its blimps flying primarily to emblazon the name Goodyear in the public eye.

Goodyear has built more than 300 airships, most of them for the armed forces. The navy formally decommissioned the last military blimp in 1964, and now Goodyear conducts blimp operations with many of the retired airships. Two of the cars on the present fleet of Goodyear blimps saw duty with the navy before Goodyear reacquired them, modified and refurbished them, and mated them to new envelopes. Although the present blimps lack some of the military electronic gear and other equipment used on navy duty, and although the engines have been changed from military to more economical civil lightplane engines, Goodyear's fleet of blimps is composed entirely of time-tested types that served the navy well.

There are four airships in Goodyear's fleet: the *Enterprise*, the *Columbia*, and the *America* operate in the United States and Canada; the *Europa* operates in Europe. The *Enterprise* recently replaced the *Mayflower*, an older design with less lifting capacity and a different envelope. Now all four Goodyear blimps are of similar design. The *Europa* is the sole exception to the rule that blimps are named after yachts that have been victorious in the America's Cup races. That rule was established by P. W. Litchfield, a former board chairman of Goodyear who believed that airships would one day fulfill the role of "air yachts" for residents of inland areas. His dream never became reality, but the naming of blimps after sailing champions has become traditional with Goodyear.

Litchfield was fascinated by airships, of course, but he was—and is—not alone. Of all aircraft shapes, that of the blimp is the most universally appealing, and it may well serve as one of humankind's most stunning examples of form following function. People who experienced a first view of the giant zeppelins, when those mammoths made their initial appearance, can still recall where they were, what they were doing, the time of day—every detail of the encounter. Few of life's experiences are so moving.

Although lighter-than-air ships once connected continents, roaming the ocean of air as the sovereigns of all vessels, we are left now with only a handful of commercial blimps; the four owned by Goodyear and a few independently owned blimps in England, Europe, and the United States. These blimps still are a far cry from the earlier giant airships that carried paying passengers and flew on schedule. The duties of today's blimps seem all frivolity by comparison, but still they fly on. They survive. While their detractors point to jumbo jets and SSTs as being more appropriate vehicles for the hurried pace of today, blimps seem as permanent as the laws of physics that declare them buoyant. They are as eternal as whimsy. And if you free your imagination for just a moment, you might fleetingly believe they are alive. □

With its ground crew in attendance, this airship lies serenely at anchor. Because blimps are vulnerable to the whims of wind, ground operations require skill.

PONY-BLIMP
FIRST 5 GOODYEAR CORDS MADE IN L.A.
FOR Douglass Fairbank's National Sextet
SOLD BY GARDEN COURT GARAGE & MOTOR SUPPLY CO.
7030 HOLLYWOOD BLVD.

2
GETTING OFF THE GROUND

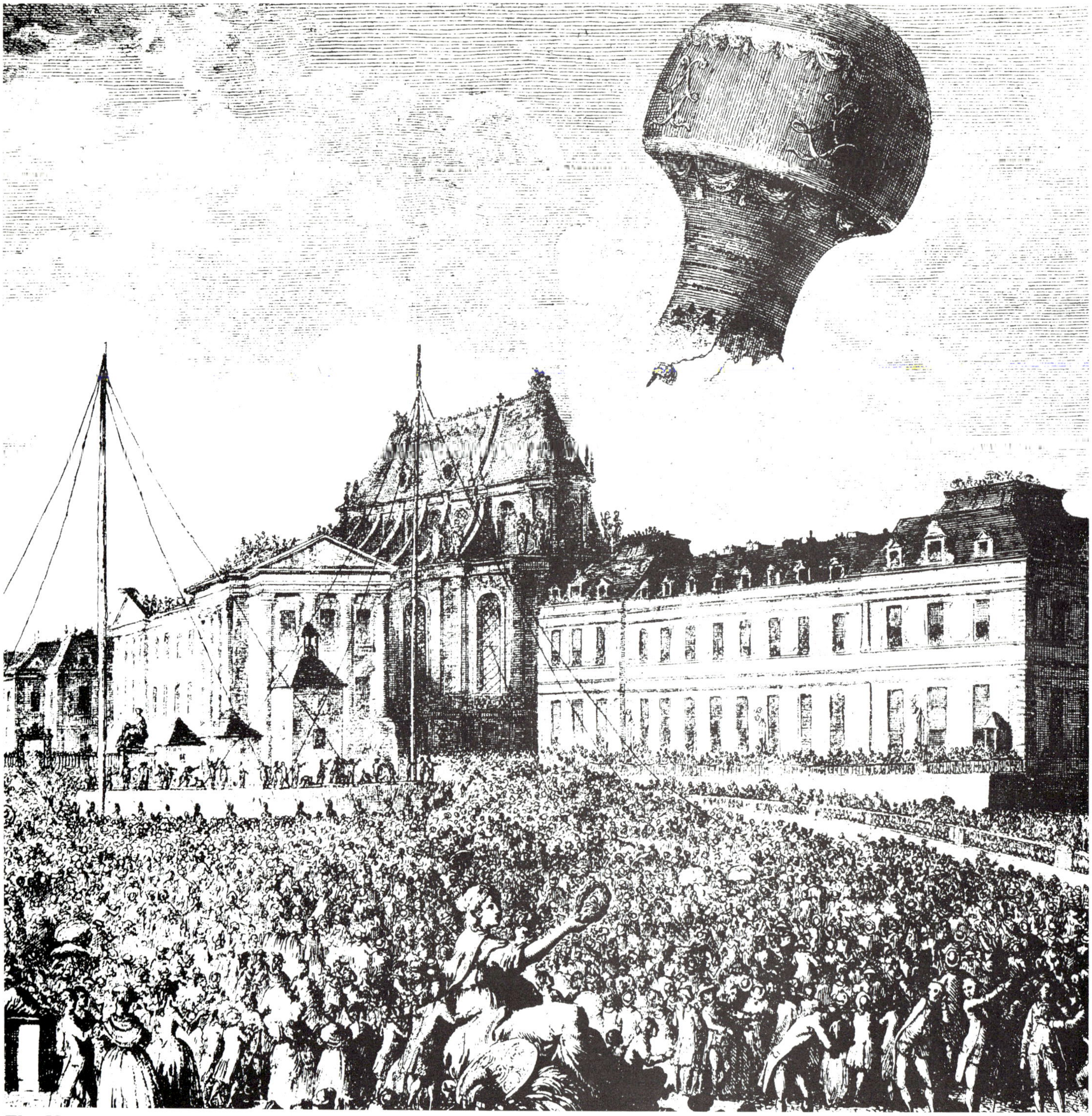

The Montgolfiers used paper balloons lifted by hot air. Here, three farm animals make the first trip aloft, at Versailles.

Almost since the first man expressed the first rational idea, flying has been a persistent human obsession. Birds made it all look annoyingly easy. From primitive drawings and other artifacts it is clear that early inventors took the direct approach: if it is meant to *fly* like a bird, then make it *look* like a bird. The history and mythology of early attempts at flight are a chronicle of failure. The complex machinery that hung from wings—some of them even designed to flap—required power that no engine yet invented could produce. So the first giddy success at flying came ultimately from an entirely different idea.

About 120 years before the Wright brothers' powered flights, another pair of aeronautically minded brothers, Joseph and Jacques Etienne Montgolfier of France, discovered a simple secret: heated air, when trapped in a lightweight container such as a paper bag, would lift a vessel and keep it aloft until the air cooled. Since the Montgolfiers were paper-makers by trade, they set about building a number of very large, spherical, paper balloons, each with a firepot suspended in a basket beneath it to keep the air hot. After several flights were made without passengers, the honor of being the first air crew went to three unlikely candidates: a sheep, a duck, and a rooster. King Louis XVI and Marie Antoinette, both of whom were present at the momentous launching from Versailles, had expressly forbidden any persons to join the animals, fearing the venture to be dangerous in the extreme. The opinions of the sheep, duck, and rooster are not a matter of record.

The flight went perfectly, though, and the animals, at least, appeared unconcerned. Following this success, the first manned flight was inevitable and imminent. Scientist Pilatre de Rozier and the Marquis d'Arlandes boarded the wicker basket on November 21, 1783, ascended, then glided on light breezes five miles to a soft landing.

In the next two years, remarkable progress was made, and balloon flights covering 150 miles in six hours were not uncommon. By 1785, Jean-Pierre Blanchard and the American Dr. Jeffries rode the wind across the English Channel. The most important single discovery during this period, however, was another made by the Montgolfiers: as a lifting agent, hydrogen was vastly superior to heated air. Hydrogen not only lifted more weight for a given volume of gas, but it could be generated conveniently at a launch site by using simple chemistry. Although hydrogen involved some risk due to its explosive flammability, its lifting properties did not expire as did those of heated air when the flame in the firepot went out. The endurance of balloons became virtually unlimited.

Soon hydrogen-filled balloons were in military use as observation vehicles, and sport balloons were a common sight in Europe and America. Their designers were the first to admit that although these balloons flew—after a fashion—they were relatively helpless baggage on the wind currents and a far cry from the purposeful flight of birds. The point was to *go* somewhere, to navigate. The new dream was of a powered balloon that could be pointed at will, even against the wind. Its fulfillment came in the form of the dirigible, which enjoyed limited success during the mid-nineteenth century. But the steam- and battery-powered electric motors used to turn its propellers were too heavy in proportion to their power output. The well-intentioned ship could be utterly immobilized by a wind of only a few miles per hour.

In 1862, as Confederate forces moved toward Washington, D.C., a physician named Solomon Andrews from Perth Amboy, New Jersey, approached government officials. Andrews proposed to turn the tide of battle with an airship he called the *Aereon,* a name of his own invention (for he was a most inventive man) that properly rang with the promise of a new aerial age. Aside from possessing credentials as an academic whiz at Yale, a medical doctor, and a former mayor and health official of Perth Amboy, Andrews had a physical presence and winning manner that overwhelmed all opposition—that is, until he encountered the government agencies of Washington, D.C. His proposal to risk his own wealth to construct the *Aereon* to fly into Confederate territory and win the war was rejected.

He returned to Perth Amboy to build the airship under his own auspices. Basically, Andrews's theory was simple: A spherical balloon would float straight up, like a cork in water. If the *Aereon* were built as a series of three cylinders joined side by side, it would behave more like a board held underwater and then released—it would tend to move laterally as it rose, thereby inducing forward motion from the lift itself. To make progress, therefore, Andrews had only to toss off

ballast with the hull pointed upward in the direction he wished to travel. At the point of maximum climb, he would valve off hydrogen and point the nose downward. A rudder provided excellent steering, and a little ballast car on tracks could be moved forward and aft to change the pitch trim and thereby raise and lower the nose. What is most remarkable about the *Aereon* is that it worked.

To the ecstasy of credible witnesses, Andrews made demonstration flights around Perth Amboy. But Honest Abe Lincoln was no visionary and he demanded the witnesses' written testimony of the feat from Andrews. In 1864, Andrews gained some ground with the government through a series of demonstration flights of small models at congressional committee hearings and the Smithsonian Institution. But before his final victory came the war's end, the death of Lincoln, and financial chaos. Although Andrews would thrill all of New York City with some spectacular flights, and even win some investors to his cause, his Aerial Navigation Company and its dream of scheduled air service failed along with the banking system. Andrews died soon afterward, but he had demonstrated that a viable dirigible design was possible, and his design even lacked an engine!

It remained for one of the most engaging and remarkable men in the history of aviation, a Brazilian dandy named Alberto Santos-Dumont, to wed the dirigible to the newly invented internal combustion engine. Santos-Dumont was born in 1873, the youngest of seven children in an aristocratic, coffee-growing family. At the peak of the Gay Nineties he moved to Paris, a city that had enchanted him on an earlier family visit.

Paris in *la belle époque* was the perfect match for the personality of Santos-Dumont. It was a city that melded the arts and sciences, possibly in a style that never has been and never will be duplicated. The Eiffel Tower and the new Impressionism in painting bespoke a spirit of adventurous experimentation in human potential. The city excited all who came there.

Alberto Santos-Dumont had a dream that possessed all his senses—the dream of flying. He was a small man, very stylish in a society that made style an art form, and there was little question that he was the darling of the café set of Paris. Still, those who knew him well reported that despite a delightful theatrical flair, he would allow almost no distraction from the construction of a series of successful airships, each of them numbered in sequence. Santos-Dumont was enthralled with machinery and comfortable with it as well. He built machines that were works of art, with the right combination of engine, rigging, and envelope.

When friends told him that the current gasoline engines, mostly used on powered tricycles, vibrated so badly that they would rip any airship into shreds, Santos-Dumont contrived an experiment. Suspending his own powered tricycle by three ropes so that it hung in midair, he climbed aboard and fired up the engine. *Voilà*! All vibration vanished, lost in the damping effect of the suspension rigging.

With similar prescience, he feared explosion not from fire igniting the hydrogen lifting gas but from the envelope rupturing as the balloon rose and the gases expanded. Expansion and loss of hydrogen during ascent nearly caused him to lose his graceful but primitive *No. 1* near Longchamps racetrack. Fortunately, some young boys caught the dangling guide ropes, turning the envelope into a kite and saving the day.

Unlike Andrews's designs, Santos-Dumont's airships were meant to conserve the lifting gas rather than valve it to provide motion. The small gasoline engine, although initially not much more than three horsepower in capacity, provided motion as well as directional control to the rudder. His ideas about the behavior of the lifting gas during flight were also quite advanced, and he devised the first appropriate mechanisms to compensate for pressure changes. By the time three more airships had followed *No. 1*, the young men of Paris unabashedly adored him, imitating even his shirt collars and his demeanor.

Then a French industrialist named Henry Deutsch offered a prize to anyone who could fly from St. Cloud to the Eiffel Tower and back again—about seven miles in all—in thirty minutes. Santos-Dumont attempted it in his advanced *No. 5*. The engine was mounted amidships on a long keel, wires replaced the ropes in order to reduce air resistance, and his own basket was mounted far out front. His first try was a failure, and so was his second, in the improved *No. 6*.

On October 19, 1901, a day plagued by a wicked wind and wretched flying conditions, Santos-Dumont launched his third attempt at the Deutsch prize. With all of Paris watch-

ing, he rounded the Eiffel Tower. Almost at that very moment, the engine died. He restarted it, but lost valuable time, crossing the finish line just thirty seconds short of the thirty-minute maximum. The crowd went wild with elation —until the judge of the event announced that at the point of landing, Santos-Dumont's time was forty seconds too long!

The city was thrown into an uproar, and even Deutsch wanted the prize awarded. In the end, a vote among members of the Aero Club awarded Santos-Dumont the money and the honors. True to his character, he donated the money to his mechanics and to the poor of Paris.

Santos-Dumont built fourteen airships in all, among them the tiny *No. 9* in which he regularly floated down to a landing in front of his favorite bistro on the Champs-Élysées. The French army's fascination with his inventions presaged an era when the airship would be more than the plaything of Paris.

By some reports, Santos-Dumont once attempted to take his own life, thinking himself responsible for a particularly gruesome airship disaster. Later he contracted a chronic disease that left him a tortured spirit. He committed suicide during the 1932 civil war in Brazil, having heard the sound of his countrymen using airplanes to drop aerial bombs upon their brothers.

If Santos-Dumont made flying stylish and blissful, some concurrent developments in southern Germany would make it awesome and fearful. There, a dedicated nobleman, Count Ferdinand von Zeppelin, captured the world's attention with the flight of a huge, sausage-shaped gasbag that bore his name. While the young Brazilian gentleman fashioned airships that were filigree delights and quite Parisian, the count built the first true ship of the air—a *Luftschiff*—to a scale that was appropriately Teutonic.

Luftschiff Zeppelin 1 (LZ-1) measured 425 feet from its blunt nose, along its parallel cylindrical hull, to the strange steering contraption on its tail. The throngs that gathered on the shore of Lake Constance in July, 1900, were awed by the enormous shape

Santos-Dumont's elegant little airships captivated the people of Paris. He finally won a prize by flying around the Eiffel Tower—but only after many failures.

Count Zeppelin built the first large airships capable of carrying commercial passengers—a brilliant technical achievement in its time.

as it slid from its hangar. This first German airship was no beauty, however.

Like his predecessors, Zeppelin was hampered by a primitive method for controlling pitch by maneuvering weights fore and aft, and his engines were more whimsical than reliable. The best that can be said of his first flight is that it averted a disaster. The LZ-1 flew for about seventeen minutes before the rigging broke and the airship settled onto the water. The rationale for using Lake Constance as a test site was thus made abundantly clear. The second and third flight of the giant sausage went little better.

Count Zeppelin, like other airship designers, was mesmerized by his vision of these giants in flight; he was immune to disappointment. With the company that had backed LZ-1 now bankrupt, Zeppelin secured permission to operate a lottery to raise funds for LZ-2. He added a sizeable piece of his own fortune to the lottery money and had the new ship ready by late 1905. It showed marked improvements in design and structure, establishing the basic triangular girder that would form the structure of all LZs thereafter. LZ-2 managed another compromise of sorts, landing after a failure in

flight, but at least demonstrating to the count that his airships could alight upon land without harm. Another lottery.

LZ-3 incorporated all the lessons and ideas that were necessary to success. It had the right combination. It flew in the autumn of 1906, and everyone in Germany, including Zeppelin's sullen antagonist, Kaiser Wilhelm, wanted a piece of the action.

LZ-4 was a magnificent work. Although it featured the first machine gun—installed in a mount atop the hull—it made only peaceful flights around Germany and Switzerland. The German government now openly acknowledged its interest in the zeppelins, and on the occasion of the LZ-4's first attempt at a twenty-four-hour flight, it dispatched official observers to report on the airship's performance. The LZ-4 performed beautifully, flying an entire day with only one brief stop.

At dawn's light, Count Zeppelin landed in a small village to organize some engine repairs. A sudden freak storm tore the huge ship loose from its mooring, with part of the crew still aboard, helpless to control it. The airship crashed into some trees and exploded in a horrible ball of fire. News of the disaster flashed across Europe, and it appeared certain that the zeppelins were finished. Among the mourners was Hugo Eckener, a writer for the *Frankfurter Zeitung*. Eckener had initially been critical of the airships, but he later turned believer and ultimately became the world's premier airship navigator as captain of a zeppelin of his own.

Zeppelin had touched the heart of his nation. Condolences poured in from everywhere and, more importantly, so did money. By 1910, only two years after the LZ-4 disaster and seven years after the first stumbling flights of the Wright brothers, huge hydrogen-filled zeppelins were flying scheduled passenger routes between major cities in Germany.

In the United States, airship sciences were not progressing nearly as rapidly as they were in Germany. In 1910, a man named Walter Wellman had tried an abortive flight across the Atlantic with an associate named Calvin Vaniman. The two argued almost from the start of their enterprise, and soon Vaniman left to build his own ship according to his own ideas. His ship was named *Akron* in honor of the head-

The giant dirigibles — now called *zeppelins* —were perverted into machines of war. This airship crew is depicted on an air raid, probably over England.

Calvin Vaniman's *Akron* was an early American attempt to build a large commercial airship. When the *Akron* blew up, efforts in the U.S. were set back for years.

quarters city of its principal backer, Goodyear.

The trouble-plagued *Akron* blew up on a 1912 flight near Atlantic City, New Jersey, killing Vaniman and leaving an indelible image in the public eye: airships were disasters waiting to happen. It would be years before another American would seriously pursue airship construction.

With the menace of war approaching in Europe, the German kaiser and his generals turned increasingly to the idea of victory through air power and were quick to recognize the potential of Count Zeppelin's invention as a powerful strategic weapon. In truth, the effectiveness of airships as high-altitude bombers had never been conclusively demonstrated, but that was held to be of little importance. The mere sight of zeppelins was thought sufficient to terrorize the enemy and thereby guarantee German victory.

Despite Zeppelin's reluctance, the airships were used as high-altitude bombers by the Imperial German armed forces during World War I. In a conflict full of nightmarish new devices of death, none had greater psychological impact than the zeppelin on the civilian populace. Suddenly, war was not a struggle fought by brave men on distant fields while their families watched and listened at a safe distance. Now there were no boundaries, no safe havens, nothing sacred. The zeppelins came at night, often concealed by clouds and navigated solely by dead reckoning. They flew so high that they could hardly be seen or heard, and they were out of range of conventional airplanes and guns. The first announcement of their arrival was often the

©
BSMITH-
ANTIC-CITY.
BB 12633

While the rest of the world could only watch, Germany experimented with such advanced air-travel ideas as shipboard transfer.

impact of their bombs.

The actual damage caused during the first airship *blitz* was minimal, due partly to the difficulties of navigating at night and partly to frequent breakdowns caused by the thin, cold air at high altitudes. Nevertheless, the zeppelins terrorized the populations of London and the industrial Midlands and greatly advanced the popular image of the ruthless, invincible Hun.

Later, more sophisticated wartime zeppelins emerged from the Friedrichshafen factories. In all, Germany built eighty-eight airships by the end of the war. The most advanced models were called "height climbers" because of their enormous gas cells and special Maybach engines that enabled them to cruise above England at altitudes of more than 20,000 feet. Airplanes of the time had great difficulty attaining even 12,000 feet. Anti-aircraft artillery had been devised accordingly and had a similar vertical range.

British aviators knew that the gasbags were vulnerable: a single incendiary bullet or tracer entering one hydrogen gas cell would cause a fire that would burn a zeppelin in seconds. Throughout the war, the British labored to improve aircraft performance, equipping several airplanes with special engines intended to close the altitude gap. On the night of August 5, 1918, the inevitable happened.

A Rolls-Royce-powered DH-5 caught the new German L-70 at the uncharacteristically low altitude of 16,500 feet. Burning machine-gun bullets found their mark, and the ship crashed with the loss of all hands, including Fregattenkapitän Peter Strasser, the charismatic and dynamic leader of the Imperial Navy's airship service. Together with staggering losses due to a storm in a previous, otherwise successful air raid in October, 1917, the incident demonstrated the vulnerability of the zeppelins, and military raids over England were suspended.

Two other events marked 1917: the death of Count Zeppelin and perhaps the most heroic flight of an airship in the entire war. On November 21, 1917, the L-59 flew from a base in Bulgaria on a desperate mission to resupply a besieged garrison in German East Africa. Although the airship was ordered to turn back only a few hundred miles from its destination, it flew for ninety-five continuous hours and covered 4,225 miles. Ironically, it was later revealed that the message to turn back had been based on a fake report stating that the outpost had been occupied by enemy forces.

Germany's defeat in the Great War led to crushing armistice terms that included the destruction of the Zeppelin company and its facilities at Friedrichshafen. In an effort to prevent the accomplishments of Count Zeppelin from passing into oblivion, the Goodyear Tire & Rubber Company entered into an agreement with Dr. Hugo Eckener, the brilliant associate who had assumed leadership of the Zeppelin organization after the count's death. Goodyear bought key zeppelin patents and incorporated a new subsidiary: the Goodyear-Zeppelin Corporation. Goodyear had built nonrigid airships and tethered barrage balloons since 1911. Now the company added the world's foremost experts and technology to its new lighter-than-air division, including Dr. Karl Arnstein, chief engineer in charge of Luftschiffbau—Zeppelin's wartime construction of rigids. The United States Navy was eager to have a fleet of modern airships that would be second to none, and Goodyear was to become its prime contractor.

In Europe, the armistice commission fortunately never carried out its threat to dismantle the former Zeppelin company, but the firm was required to build several ships as reparations for the victors. From this program the United States Navy acquired the LZ-126, which it christened the U.S.S. *Los Angeles*. The navy had already copied a captured zeppelin that had landed in France, naming this copy the *Shenandoah*.

Finally, the Germans were free to set to work on LZ-127, destined to become the legendary airship of all time—the *Graf Zeppelin*. From its conception, the *Graf* was designed to be a commercial passenger airship. Eckener, who probably shared the old count's aversion to war, envisioned a fleet of such airships providing rapid, comfortable service between Europe, America, the Far East, and South America. The *Graf Zeppelin* was to be the machine that would point the way for future travelers and investors. At 755 feet, it was the longest and largest airship yet built. Its first flight was made in September, 1928, and less than a year later it stunned a world that was still reeling from Lindbergh's solo Atlantic flight by flying around the globe with a full load of passengers and making only three stops: Tokyo, Los Angeles, and New York.

The amazing *Graf* then settled into the routine it would follow for several years, making scheduled round trips between Germany and Brazil. In flight, the airship averaged over seventy miles per hour while the passengers dined regally, retired to comfortable and beautifully appointed staterooms, or stood at wide promenade windows that could be opened en route for a better view of the land- and seascapes passing 1,000 feet below.

The U.S. Navy built a fleet of airships, like the *Shenandoah* (above), based on the Germans' rigids. Although the early blimps were dwarfed by rigids, they would ultimately prevail.

The loss of the *Hindenburg* ended the dream of long-distance airship travel envisioned by Dr. Hugo Eckener, shown at left with American airship commander Charles E. Rosendahl.

If there was one nagging problem allied with airships, it was the persistent fear of a hydrogen fire. But the competent airshipmen of DELAG, the German airline that operated these flying liners, took extensive safety precautions. For example, all smoking materials, including matches, were turned over to the stewards at the start of a flight. En route, a passenger desiring a cigar or pipe was politely shown to a special parlor where a crew member provided a cautious light.

In 1936, a new and much larger German zeppelin was put into commercial service. Christened the *Hindenburg*, the 803-foot behemoth was put into scheduled passenger service between Germany and New York. The ship was far more elegant than the *Graf*, carrying seventy passengers in airborne luxury that is unequalled to this day. Since the war, the German ships had rung up an unblemished safety record, but hydrogen as a lifting gas was a continuing, shadowy threat to the perpetuation of that record. Thus, the decision had been made to use helium, a completely inert lifting gas, as a substitute for the unstable hydrogen. The *Hindenburg* had been designed accordingly.

The decision was complicated by two factors: the United States had the world's only known source of commercial helium; and the Nazis, now in control of Germany, were the subject of great political debate in the United States. The expectation of another war in Europe was nearly universal, and the government of the United States, possibly fearing military use of the helium, barred its sale to Germany. Given no alternative source of supply, the Germans inflated the *Hindenburg* with hydrogen.

On the evening of May 6, 1937, as the *Hindenburg* was making a routine landing at Lakehurst, New Jersey, after a flight from Germany, fire suddenly broke out near the tail. Within seconds, the entire length of the ship settled to the ground in flames. Journalists, routinely on hand for zeppelin landings, recorded the catastrophe in gruesome detail for radio, newspaper, and newsreel audiences. Thirty-six people died in the conflagration. Although anti-Nazi sabotage has long been presumed to have caused the disaster and the evidence seems to support that conclusion overwhelmingly, no official explanation of exactly what went wrong has ever been made.

The loss of the *Hindenburg* effectively ended the dream of globe-girdling commercial airship service, perhaps forever. Its sister ship, *Graf Zeppelin*, on a return trip from Brazil at the time of the disaster, was put into the Friedrichshafen hangar upon its arrival and never flew with another paying passenger. A newly completed *Graf Zeppelin II* made a number of flights over Germany in the late 1930s, but when World War II broke out both ships were unceremoniously dismantled so that other uses could be made of their valuable aluminum. From that time on, the mantle of dominance of the world's airship fleet passed to the United States.

In fact, the *Hindenburg*'s was not the only disastrous airship accident, and it is a distortion of history to blame that ship alone for the end of the era of rigids. No nation that launched an airship of any size was untouched by accidents and tragedy. The English, in particular, knew the pain of disaster. In the mid-1920s Great Britain's empire ranged over the entire world. What better way to tie it together in the new age than with a fleet of airships? Britain's navy already dominated the seas, and now the nation would assert itself in the skies as well.

But that goal was to become mired in the political maneuverings of the day. As a result of internal bickering, a compromise solution was reached in which two airships were built, one by the Vickers company, to be called the R-100, and the other, to be called the R-101, by the government team of designers who had only recently built the R-38, a rigid that had broken up and crashed with heavy loss of life, due to structural failure. Remarkably, not one of the engineers responsible for the fiasco had been censured. They were to perpetuate their ignorance in the new airship.

The R-101 was a bad airship from the day it was designed. Later inquiries would reveal that elementary calculations concerning structural strength had never been made. The airship was heavy, underpowered, and, as its crew discovered to their horror, its skin had rotted as the result of an unforeseen chemical reaction! The privately built R-100, though perhaps not as well-designed as the airship that the Germans turned out, was at least airworthy and, after a series of flight trials in 1930, performed a smooth demonstration flight to Canada and back.

The builders of the R-101 were under contractual obligation to perform a similar long-distance demonstration flight, but theirs would be to India and back. England's air minister, one Baron Thomson, wanted to accompany the flight for his own political purposes, and he pressed for the earliest possible departure. His haste and greed for publicity may have deterred the builders from making necessary modifications.

Even if the builders had benefited from more time, though, the R-101 seemed beset by a cumulative series of errors that virtually doomed the airship's October attempt to reach India. Outward bound while crossing the countryside of France, it literally burst in the stress of a storm. Only six survived, and Baron Thomson was not among them. Thus, in 1930, England's enthusiasm for an airship fleet was brought to an abrupt end.

Italy produced its own semirigid, christened the *Italia*, as part of an effort to explore the Arctic wastes. This ship featured a rigid structural keel, which hung beneath a nonrigid bag similar to that of a blimp's. In 1928, during bad weather and in difficult flying conditions, the airship struck an Arctic ice formation and broke up. The accident led to one of the most heroic rescue operations ever undertaken. Some of the crew were found and saved after days on an ice floe, but the search for the ship itself and for six crew members who had vanished along with it was finally abandoned.

Thus, nation after nation pursued the dream of a floating air fleet that would span oceans. The tragic results, along with the steady improvement in airplane performance and reliability, would eventually lead to the abandonment of lighter-than-air on the grounds that it was a principle inherently vulnerable to the weather.

The ultimate agonies were played out in rigid airships by none other than the United States Navy. In the end, the U.S. Navy would itself turn away from the rigids and embrace blimps, finally disproving the prejudices against airships, only to abandon altogether the application of airships to the waging of war.□

The British R-100 (near right) and R-101 (facing page) were rivals for an airship design that was meant to extend the empire's reach. But the loss of the R-101 put an end to the dream.

U.S.NAVY
104
108
109
110
U.S.NAVY
112
114
116
117
118
120

3
THE EYES OF THE FLEET

On June 1, 1915, the United States Navy awarded $45,636.25 to the Connecticut Aircraft Company for the design and construction of the navy's first airship, to be listed as the DN-1 (it was later redesignated the A-1). As is so often the case in the aviation business, the first company to win a contract was not the one that endured. Connecticut lasted through a number of new contracts for improved B-class airships in 1917, but its rivals were the giant B.F. Goodrich (yes, contrary to what you may think, there *was* a Goodrich blimp) and the Goodyear Tire & Rubber Company. Connecticut's DN-1 made three flights, was deflated, and never flew again, according to official naval archives.

In 1918, the launching of an airplane from the new C-1 airship near Mineola, Long Island, not only made good newspaper copy, full of fantasies of the future, but hinted at the navy's plans for its airships. These were times of vigorous interservice competition, and the army was pursuing its own adventuresome schemes in fixed-wing aircraft.

In 1919, the international race for air supremacy culminated in a dash across the Atlantic that was sponsored by the London *Daily Mail*. Among the favorites were some U.S. Navy fixed-wing flying boats of the NC type, built by Curtiss, and the German navy's mighty L-72 under the command of Kapitän Ernst Lehmann. On May 15, an unannounced entry arrived at Newfoundland with the declared intention of trying for Ireland: it was the U.S. Navy's little C-5, a nonrigid airship that amazed everyone by making the distance from Montauk, Long Island, to Newfoundland—some 1,022 miles—in only twenty-five hours and fifty minutes.

While the comparatively tiny blimp rode at anchor before leaving Newfoundland for Ireland, the NC flying boats were scheduled to depart for the Azores, setting up yet another rivalry within the navy itself—between the heavier-than-air and lighter-than-air proponents—that would persist for decades. The C-5 had landed in calm weather, but without warning, a gusty storm arose and soon threatened the airship. Hoping to gather the crew in time to cast off and avoid a wreck at anchor, two ground-crew officers climbed aboard the bucking car and attempted to ride out the sudden bursts of wind, which grew so strong they began to break up the car and propeller. When a last-ditch attempt to rip open the envelope and deflate the ship failed, the two officers gave the straining ground crew a final command to release the handling lines, then they jumped to the ground. The C-5 rose and vanished in the wind. It was never seen again.

It was no surprise, therefore, when the secretary of the navy approved plans for construction of something thought to be less risky. The Germans seemed to have the knack for airship design, judging by the success of the zeppelins; the navy ordered a virtual copy of the captured L-49, which had landed with little damage in France during an air raid. This first rigid airship for the navy was duly designed from the German specifications and named the U.S.S. *Shenandoah* with the designation ZR-1.

One of Italy's semirigids arrived in 1919 and served in the United States Navy for

Whether the bomb visible on the rear of the car on this early U.S. Navy airship was real or just dummy is open to question; at least the crewmen look purposeful.

about three months, but it performed poorly. It was deflated and work continued on the *Shenandoah*. By 1921, the first naval airship station that deserved the name was commissioned at Lakehurst, New Jersey—a town that would become a center for airship nostalgia in the years to follow. In that same year a second rigid, the ZR-2, was completed by the British for delivery to the Americans; its British designation was R-38.

R-38 never made it. A structural deficiency caused it to snap in two during its third trial flight, burning and spilling its crew into the Humber River in one of the worst air disasters on record. It was some time before the truth behind the tragedy emerged.

While the British had gained a worldwide reputation by breaking several speed and distance records with the predecessor R-34, that ship had concealed a vast ignorance of airship design. R-38 had been cobbled up out of estimates of the zeppelin designs with the insertion of a center bay for additional gas. This modification completely destroyed the airship's control dynamics, and one attempt at high-speed flight showed conclusively that it was unstable. During that flight, some middle girders were snapped, and the airship was put up for repairs.

Instead of accepting the disappointment of a simple error, however, the builders compounded their mistake by doubling the rigidity of the structure in the area they repaired. Any engineer knows that a unit structure like a dirigible cannot be built with any single portion significantly stronger than the rest, lest it become a point of stress concentration. That was exactly what happened over the Humber River.

Still, the U. S. Navy pursued its plan for a fleet of giant rigids, and who can fault them? These giants were so much more impressive than the little nonrigid blimps, which made their own quiet progress, virtually ignored. Shortly after the R-38 crashed, a navy blimp, the C-7, became the first airship to fly with helium as the lifting gas, a milestone of progress that gained scant attention. Through the early 1920s, the navy plodded along on its own, opening a training school for airship pilots and crew, and all the while operating its two rigids, the *Shenandoah* and *Los Angeles*. The latter was built by the Zeppelin works according to tried and tested German principles, all of which had been learned the hard way.

The Americans continued experimenting with all forms of new operations. After miraculously surviving a storm that wrenched the nose anchor from the airship, the *Shenandoah* was repaired and flown in trials designed to test mooring operations at sea. In 1925, tragedy struck again. The *Shenandoah,* on a Midwest tour that had originally been scheduled for the *Los Angeles,* flew into a system of thunderstorms and line squalls over Ava, Ohio. Battered by the turbulence, the airship's long hull snapped like a foundering sea vessel caught between swells. Its back broken, the *Shenandoah* fell in two pieces. The rear portion crashed to earth while the forward section, flying like a free balloon with its crew clinging to what remained of its structure, eventually came to rest in a farmyard. Among the survivors was its navigator, Charles Rosendahl, who would later rise to the very peak of the navy's airship command.

It was apparent that the eager Americans, while filled with zeal and optimism, lacked the countless hours of flying experience which had enabled their German counterparts to cope so well in similar crises caused by bad weather. While Dr. Hugo Eckener flew the world skirting storms, American navy pilots seemed determined to plunge into their darkest centers.

In fairness, it must be said

Although the extraordinary all-metal ZMC-2 (near right) was said to have been an efficient airship, the crowd at the *Akron's* christening at Goodyear in August, 1931 (facing page), indicates the navy's real interest—large rigids.

The *Akron* set a world record in November, 1931, by carrying 207 passengers on a single flight, a feat that was not duplicated by an airplane for decades.

that the American pilots may have been right in their belief that until airships could be demonstrated to survive the heaviest weather, they could not be used with confidence as machines of war. And there is some circumstantial evidence to suggest that their flying may not have been at the root of the problem. Deviations from the Germans' structural principles may have at least partially contributed to the accidents.

In 1929, one curiosity briefly emerged: On August 19, a strange, egg-shaped airship designated ZMC-2 was launched. The Z stood for "zeppelin," but the *MC* was startling—this was the navy's first and last metal-clad airship. Built by Aircraft Development Corporation, an independent firm, the ZMC-2 may well have been ahead of its time. Even its construction prefigured the advanced techniques that would one day be applied to airplanes. Built section by section while suspended on end, the aluminum shell of the airship was literally stitched together by a unique new method employing rows of tiny rivets.

Unfortunately, companies such as Lakewood Airships and Aircraft Development Corporation simply could not endure the Byzantine workings of navy contracts, and although the ZMC-2 was said by those who had flown it to be a surprisingly efficient airship, it was abandoned, and the major attention continued to be directed toward Akron and Goodyear. In 1931, in fact, Goodyear completed its third huge rigid, named *Akron* by the navy. This ship set a record in November of the same year by transporting 207 persons on a ten-hour flight, the greatest

U.S

The daring young navy men called "trapeze artists" operated small fighters from a base aboard the rigid airships (above). A hook on the airplane engaged the "trapeze" on the fly (facing page).

number of passengers ever carried aboard an airship.

Two years later, the *Akron* was lost, and along with it the life of the U.S. Navy's most stalwart proponent of lighter-than-air craft, Admiral William A. Moffett. Again, weather played a role; the new *Akron* was destroyed off the New Jersey coast in a thunderstorm at night. According to the survivors' reconstruction of events leading up to the final moments, the flight was notable only for being routine. There was the storm, yes, but there had been storms before. This time, the airship just seemed to fall into the sea. Compounding the disaster, a small nonrigid, the J-3, was lost while searching for survivors of the *Akron*. Only seventeen days later, the ZRS-5, named the U.S.S. *Macon*, was commissioned amid doubts about airships among the navy's airmen. The final blow to the navy's romance with rigids would soon fall.

The *Macon* was identical to its sister ship, the *Akron*, but among its crew there was no fear of linked fates. Much had been learned from past mistakes, and if nothing else the *Macon* at least had the benefit of adequate life rafts and rescue training for the crew. From the beginning, this giant 785-foot rigid seemed blessed. In war games, the crew had demonstrated persuasively that a navy equipped with airships would have the upper hand in a battle encounter with any enemy unlucky enough to lack the "eyes" of the *Macon*, a small fleet of scout airplanes.

The airship carried its fleet in an internal hangar, from which it launched and recovered the small biplanes with a device called a trapeze (which led to the pilots being known as "trapeze artists"); it could also hide in a cloud bank and lower a small car with an observer inside to telephone enemy positions and movements. The crew was sharp, and in test after test they had proven the worth of navy tactical doctrine. In Washington and Lakehurst, the lighter-than-air faction began to sense the comfort of success. At last, the rigid airship was playing a key role—just as they had envisioned it would.

To what extent this enthusiasm contributed to the end of the *Macon* is debatable, but after the loss of the *Akron*, and with the *Los Angeles* now decommissioned, everyone in the navy wanted the remaining *Macon* everywhere at once. Racing across the southwestern United States to complete an assignment in the Caribbean, the ship encountered turbulence strong enough to snap some structure in the tail. The crew made temporary repairs with wooden splints, and permanent repairs were dragged out between flights so that the valuable airship could continue participation in maneuvers.

Back at home base on the Pacific Coast, the *Macon* spent a day of successful operations with the fleet and was headed back to the hangar for more overhaul work when a storm suddenly punished the airship with strong wind gusts. Those who witnessed the final moments of the *Macon* described the virtual disintegration of the control surfaces near the tail. Now helpless, the great ship could only prolong the agony before a final plunge to the ocean surface. All but two of the crew escaped this time, but after the fall of the *Macon* no more rigids were built.

The *Macon* was lost in February, 1935. In October of that same year, the navy purchased the ten-passenger *Defender* from Goodyear. This

airship had been built in 1929 and represented the quiet progress Goodyear had been making all the while in nonrigid technology. *Defender* became U.S. Navy airship G-1 and in 1937 was followed by the purchase of L-1 and K-2. The L ships were comparatively small and formed the core of the training fleet throughout World War II. The Ks would become the workhorse class of the lighter-than-air fleet.

Throughout 1942 and 1943, Goodyear-Zeppelin delivered airships as fast as it could make them, while the navy began an intensive training buildup for war. Along both coasts, naval air stations were built virtually overnight, and the new coastal patrol blimps went on station. Their mission: the detection of enemy submarines.

Although the record of the blimps has been overshadowed by more dramatic events of greater intensity, two facts about the blimp fleet stand out: with the switch to nonrigids, the navy never again suffered the calamitous losses that had characterized its flirtation with rigids; and, throughout the duration of World War II, *no vessel escorted by blimps was ever lost to enemy submarine action.* The strategic impact of this accomplishment, achieved in an operation that could be described as so routine as to be boring, is difficult to convey.

On July 18, 1943, a blimp on patrol off the Florida coast encountered a German submarine running on the surface. The airship's commander, Nelson Grills, opted to attack the submarine, to his ultimate regret. The sub peppered the blimp's envelope with its machine guns and forced a water landing. The sub was later found and sunk by surface ships. The K-74 was lost, though it found a place in history as the only blimp ever to duel with a submarine.

Despite that lone aberration, the navy's doctrine on the use of blimps in combat was basic caution. Their low speed and large size were a liability, whereas their tremendous range and endurance were definite assets. By 1944, navy blimp operations had spread out to South America and to the Mediterranean, where Squadron 14 operated the first airships in the European theater.

With the war's end, air stations and squadrons were decommissioned as fast as they had sprung up. The navy's great fleet of K ships dispersed, some to the Coast Guard and others to be attached to various fleets under new command.

The postwar period was a time of great experimentation during which the full capabilities of blimps were explored. Although this peacetime era is often described as one of tedium—and there is no question it was—the navy was not dragging its anchor. In 1946 the new XM-1 blimp set a duration record of 170.3 hours, the first of many records that were to follow. The expanding antisubmarine role for blimps called for long-range operations from carrier decks and in weather conditions that had previously grounded the airships.

In June, 1951, a prototype for a new, modern class of blimps emerged. The ZPG-1 was an enormous aircraft, larger than any previous non-

When the blimps took over convoy surveillance, their deterrence was so effective that not a single vessel was ever lost in a convoy they escorted. Still, the navy doubted their worth.

THE MASTER NAVIGATOR

Jack Hunt is no ordinary man. For one thing, he is an airship pilot, a profession that sets one apart. But there is something extraordinary to his character that would probably have led him to achieve more than his peers no matter what the undertaking.

Hunt fit the navy's round hole like a square peg. He was a reservist among regular officers, innocent of the creeping inertia that comes over careerists. Stationed in Florida as a young airshipman, he was not so much a renegade as a grating presence, continually urging the navy to *do* something with its blimps. Those around him thought the blimps were doing just fine moored to their masts. It was not long before he found his way to South Weymouth, his reputation preceding him.

His new station commander was cool toward him until the day Hunt cajoled him into a free-balloon training ride (all navy blimp pilots were required to learn free ballooning prior to training in powered blimps) that ended in one of Hunt's patented pinpoint landings in an open field. The commander was impressed.

Hunt and others of his ilk turned South Weymouth into an all-weather operation at a time when the navy had grave fears about airship operations in such conditions. The public was unaccustomed to blimps as well. On one occasion, when a South Weymouth airship dangled its control car over a reservoir in Massachusetts in order to take on water for ballast, civilians on the ground thought they had witnessed the first interplanetary visit. Cut out that stuff, ordered the navy. From then on, the blimps took their ballast from the ocean and frightened only fishermen, who were miles from a phone.

When the idea first arose to make the Atlantic flight in the *Snowbird,* Hunt was already an accomplished airship commander, with experience in heavy weather, including icing and thunderstorms. He had also already performed trial flights for the National Advisory Committee for Aeronautics to determine how a blimp would fly if the ballonets were unable to do their job. In these so-called "limp bag" trials, Hunt flew a blimp with the envelope pressure severely reduced. The loss of pressure so distorted the shape of the blimp that its control surfaces were no longer aligned with its axis: like a banana, the airship curved upward at nose and tail. Hunt demonstrated that, instead of flying forward, the blimp would constantly attempt to climb because of the misalignment between its nose and tail surfaces, with the resulting flight a series of stalls—short climbs followed by fall-offs.

Unlike a career officer, Hunt wanted only to say farewell to the navy, to get his job over with, and to pursue other, more civilian, ambitions. After World War II, he had flown an airship for Howard Hughes, who briefly operated a blimp to publicize his new star, Jane Russell, in her motion picture debut, *The Outlaw.* Hunt was well known around Los Angeles and the West Coast in those years as a competent, though recalcitrant, blimp pilot. Douglas Leigh, another Californian operating commercial surplus blimps, acquired one airship that got caught in a surprise snowstorm in Los Angeles. In a panic—for the ship was in serious trouble—one of Leigh's associates begged Hunt to help them out. Hunt drove to the mooring site and lashed the blimp's rip-cord to a car. Then, in a feat of consummate timing, he cast the blimp loose while signaling the driver to speed ahead and pull the cord to deflate the envelope. The maneuver worked perfectly: the blimp deflated and settled, and when the crew examined it for damage they found only four broken lightbulbs in the night sign.

Hunt had a kind of supreme confidence that melded swagger and insouciance; were that not the case, the *Snowbird* flight might never have happened. Given permission to take his idea to Washington, Hunt was told that if he could get the approval of eight admirals, he could make the flight. In the United States Navy at that time, such a requirement was tantamount to a dead end. Any reasonable person would have given Hunt long odds at getting even one approval in a year's time. He came back with all eight signatures in a single day—an achievement that may have rivaled the *Snowbird* flight itself.

Jack Hunt went on to innovate ideas for antisubmarine tactics and to persuade others to his way of thinking. He espoused the principle of "clear lanes"—seaways kept free of submarines through combined use of airships, sensors, and advanced weapons. He considered the notion of randomly routed convoys to be outmoded. In his final years in the navy, he became embroiled in disputes with some of the airship designers over the flying qualities of blimps that were being assembled by men who never had to fly in them.

Jack R. Hunt is now Dr. Hunt, president of Embry-Riddle Aeronautical University in Daytona Beach, Florida. He has brought the same spirit of achievement to this job that he brought to flying blimps, and today, Embry-Riddle graduates, who refer to him in respectful and somewhat awe-struck tones as "President Hunt," are running airlines and flight operations all over the world. Chances are the pilot of the next airliner you fly can tell you all about Jack Hunt.

Airshipmen of all nations still turn to Hunt for the answers to the tough questions, for he alone has been there and back, not once but many times. No airship pilot in the world today has Hunt's savvy or his extensive experience flying large airships. History recognizes only a few great geniuses of airship navigation: Count Zeppelin, Hugo Eckener, and Jack Hunt.

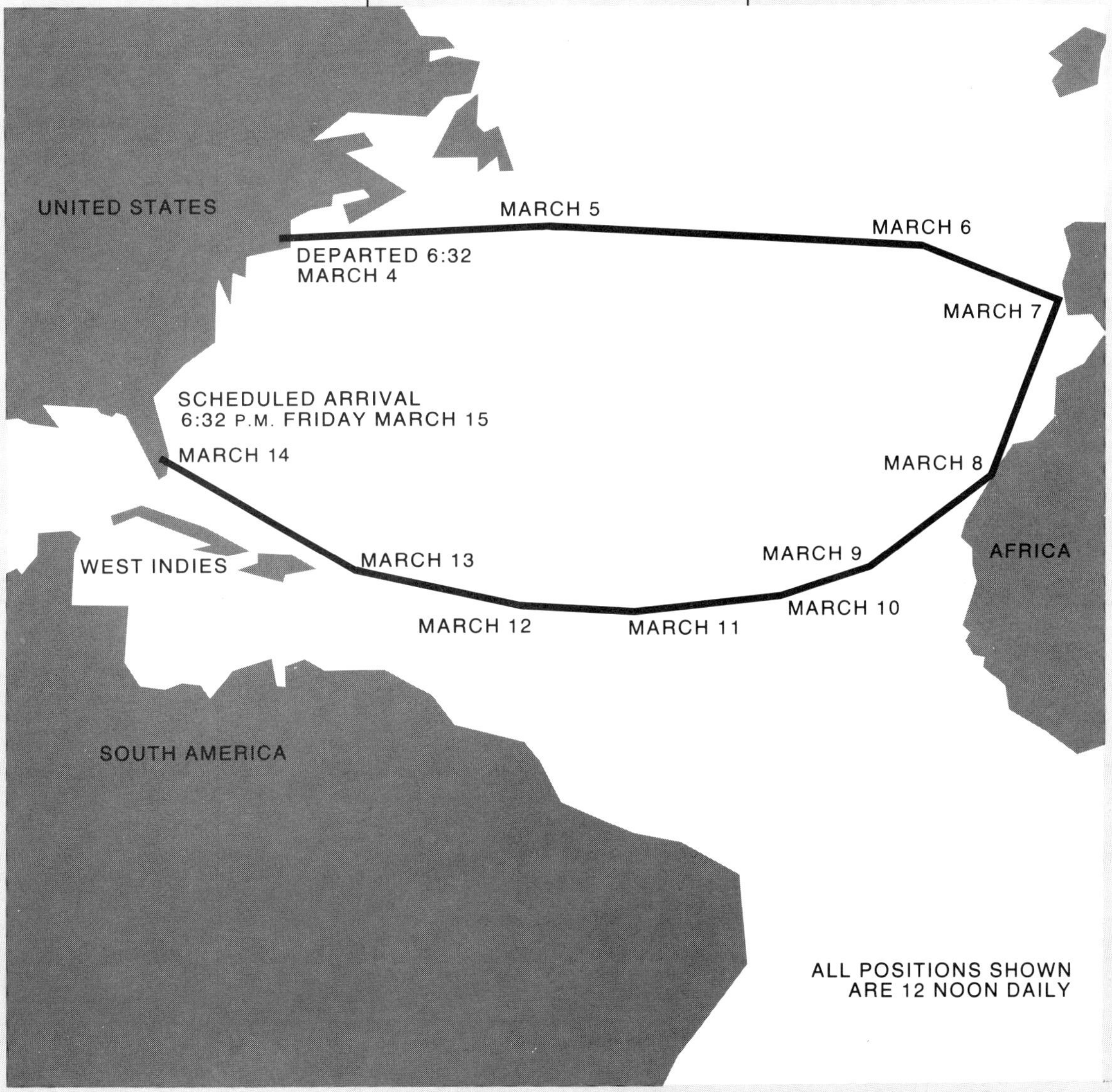

The incredible eleven-day odyssey of the *Snowbird* was made without a single stop to refuel or resupply. The flight has never been equaled by any aircraft. It revealed the blimp's best quality: endurance.

4

CLOSEUP: HOW IT WORKS

This fascinating machine called a blimp is both simple and complex: simple in principle, complex in refinement. It is the outgrowth of an intriguing natural phenomenon—that a bag filled with gas lighter than the surrounding air will rise and float across the land.

The earliest balloons used heated air as their light gas. Today's hot-air balloons employ the same technique, though their bags are now made of strong, synthetic fabrics and propane burners replaced firepots as air heaters.

German zeppelins and the large airships that copied their designs obtained their lift from millions of cubic feet of hydrogen, the lightest and most plentiful element in the universe. Yet despite its abundance, hydrogen is not the preferred lifting gas because it needs only the tiniest spark in the presence of air to touch off the type of explosion and fire that ended the career of the *Hindenburg* and terminated the shining promise of the zeppelins.

The Americans switched to helium even before the *Hindenburg* disaster. All the Goodyear blimps still use helium, a gas that is so slightly heavier than hydrogen that the difference is difficult to measure. Helium is one of a family of elements called inert gases. Do anything you like to helium, but you will get no bang, no fire, no nothing. It is comforting to know that above the gondola of the blimp is one of the world's safest known substances. Literally *nothing* can happen to helium.

Helium is found primarily in the United States in certain deposits of natural gas located mainly in Texas and Kansas. Since helium will not burn, the gas companies separate it from the flammable methane gas they pump out to customers. To these companies, helium is merely an annoying impurity: to an airship, it is the breath of life. Goodyear's airships are each filled with more than 200,000 cubic feet of this rare gas. That amount is sufficient

Birth of a blimp: the inflation of an envelope must be carefully coordinated. Ballast nets prevent the bag from floating away before the weight of the car can be affixed.

GOOD

Control surfaces (top) are secured by cables; longer lines connect to the pilot's controls. The shiny "jet" (bottom) is a turbine generator that powers the night sign.

engines shut down.

When the pilot wishes to deflate the ballonets somewhat by releasing some of their contained air, he can open a valve at the base of the envelope to dump air out of the ballonet above it. Deflating the forward ballonet and inflating the aft one will trim the blimp by squeezing the helium forward, thus lifting the nose. Pushing the helium back by reversing the process will lighten the tail. By monitoring the total inflation of both ballonets, the pilots can control the pressure of the helium itself. You can think of the ballonets as balloons within a balloon. If the smaller balloons within the larger one are inflated, the pressure increases inside the bigger balloon, too. Using this system, the blimp can fly up to about 3,000 feet above sea level and compensate for the expansion of the helium at the lower pressure at that altitude simply by allowing the ballonets to collapse. No helium need be vented, no expensive gas lost.

Modern nonrigid airships maintain their shape solely by means of the pressure within the bag. Most blimp envelopes are made by Goodyear from a Dacron fabric coated with neoprene—a tough, flexible, synthetic rubber. It does not take much pressure to inflate the envelope—about enough to push back an inch and a half of water—and when it is fully inflated, it is tight, strong, and wrinkle-free.

The gondola—the car hanging below the bag—looks as if it is fastened to the bottom. In fact, it hangs from the *top* of the envelope. A system of steel cables suspends the roof of the gondola from two *catenary curtains* sewed into the topmost fabric of the envelope. If you are flying above a blimp and looking down at it, you can see two ridges in the envelope where the curtains exert their pull. Very early blimps had catenary systems on the outside of the envelope where they were easier to see. But all that rigging also gathered ice or created drag in the air during flight, so modern blimps have internal curtains.

The tail fins work like the feathers of an arrow to control the direction of flight. They are anchored to the envelope at their bases and supported in position by guy wires. The elevators and rudders are mounted with hinges on the trailing edges of these fins. By flipping up or down, left or right, they can control the pitch and direction of the blimp. Cables connect the elevators—the surfaces that move the nose up or down—to a large wheel at the pilot's right and the rudders to two huge pedals, which he controls with his feet as if he were pumping an old air-organ. Other cables run from the gondola to the various vents and dampers that control air in the ballonets.

Mounted on the blimp's red aluminum nose cone is a large ball like the ones found on trailer hitches. This ball engages with latches on the mooring mast to anchor the blimp. Behind the nose cone, hollow aluminum tubes radiate back within laces. These *battens* help to reinforce the nose, which has to take a lot of strain when the blimp is moored. A strong wind will actually cause the blimp to elongate visibly, and you can watch the track of its single wheel change as the wind stretches the envelope.

The mast is designed to hold

The nose cone is reinforced by tubes called battens laced into the envelope. At the cone's tip is a latching mechanism similar to a trailer hitch. Mooring the blimp is a painstaking operation.

the blimp firmly in winds of even hurricane force, and it has done so more than once. But should the airship somehow wrench itself free from the hitch, it will not get far. Sewn into the top of the envelope is a twenty-two foot zipperlike device called a *rip-panel*. This panel is connected by a rope to the top of the mast whenever the blimp is moored so that the ship will tear itself open and deflate if it should accidentally break away. This is a last-ditch emergency measure, but it works.

Goodyear manufactures its envelopes at a facility in Arizona, while the blimps themselves are assembled and inflated in the Houston hangar. A blimp has a life expectancy of about six years before the envelope will have aged to the point when it begins to leak helium. The cars have no limit to their useful lives. Most of them have actually been in service since World War II, though periodically they are completely refurbished.

The blimp's two engines are similar to those found on light airplanes, except that they have been mounted backward to push instead of pull with their propellers. The props are reversible, which is a good thing, since they are the only way to stop a blimp. No brakes!

The blimps cruise at about thirty-five miles per hour, with an all-out top speed of a little over fifty. Of course, the wind has a lot to do with the airship's speed over the ground on a trip from one place to another. A thirty-five mile-per-hour headwind would stop the airship in its tracks, while that same wind on the tail would send it galloping along at seventy.

If they are flown economically, these blimps can stay in the air for twenty-four hours on a full load of fuel. Such a flight can become uncomfortable, however, since there are no restrooms or kitchen facilities aboard.

The total lift from a given volume of helium can be affected by as many variables as the stock market—temperature, atmospheric pressure, humidity, altitude, and purity of the gas itself are among the elements in the equation.

Although the blimps are called "lighter-than-air" craft, they usually operate with enough ballast to make them slightly heavier than "EQ" (that is crew talk for the *equilibrium* condition wherein the blimp neither rises nor sinks but floats perfectly mo-

The crew chief (near right) is using hand signals to tell the pilot "raise the nose," "keep it coming," and "nose to the left." A portable wind sock (facing page) helps the pilot land precisely into the surface wind.

GOODYEAR

The large wheel to the pilot's right (top) controls the elevators. On some flights the ground crew bounces the blimp on its wheel, then tosses it upward and lets go (bottom).

tionless in the air). The blimp's forward motion through the air will produce enough dynamic lift to compensate for a slightly heavy condition. The blimp's envelope is shaped like an airfoil of an airplane's wing, and the dynamic lift it produces is similar to an airplane's lift. By increasing its angle of attack into the air passing by as it flies forward, it can maintain altitude even with an extremely heavy overload of fuel for a long flight. Of course, it must maintain its forward motion in order to continue flying under those conditions. In fact, Goodyear blimps can fly as much as 800 pounds heavy on the rare occasion, such as a long cross-country assignment, that calls for a great deal of equipment and fuel. A truly heavy takeoff requires a rolling technique similar to the technique used by airplanes, with the blimp trundling down the runway on its single wheel. When the ship is operating in its normal range, the typical takeoff weight is 100 to 200 pounds heavy and the airship usually is tossed into the air—literally—by the crew. The pilot then advances the throttles and continues upward on momentum and thrust.

There is no great trick to estimating the heaviness or lightness of a blimp. A good rule of thumb says that for every pound of weight the blimp will sink one foot per minute; therefore, 100 pounds heavy yields a 100-feet-per-minute sink rate. If it were light by 100 pounds, it would *rise* instead of sinking. An experienced crew chief can estimate a blimp's weight, or lack of it, by ordering his crew to raise the ship until the handrail of the gondola is at shoulder height. When they let go, he watches what happens. Shotbags, each containing 25 pounds of lead, are added to or removed from a bin in the bottom of the gondola as the pilot and crew chief direct. Once they are satisfied with the ship's weight, the pilot signals the airshipman's traditional command to cast off—"Up ship!"—and the crew on the handrail lift the blimp once more, let it drop and bounce on its wheel, and then finally heave it aloft as if it were a huge medicine ball.

The blimp climbs at a startling angle, its engines roaring as it scrambles for altitude. About a thousand feet above sea level is typical for cruising. Then the engines are throttled back and the airship settles in for the flight. One odd thing about these airships is that they do everything—climb, cruise, dive—at the same speed: about thirty-five miles per hour. Pilots of heavier-than-air craft are usually surprised by these weird characteristics, particularly the steep takeoff angle. Once accustomed to it, however, they cannot stop smiling; no airplane can be handled with such abandon.

Landing is a more complex operation than takeoff. If the helium has been heated by the sun and a lot of fuel has burned off, the blimp may be hundreds of pounds lighter than it was at takeoff. A light ship tends to float and it must be driven to the ground, nose down, engines thrashing away at high power—holding the unwilling beast to earth—until the crew can hurl enough ballast aboard to keep it down for good.

The most important factor on the approach is the direc-

With upward momentum supplied by the ground crew, the pilot adds full throttle—and away they go. The steep climb angle surprises experienced airplane pilots.

tion of the wind, for the blimp must land exactly into it. Any amount of sideward drift makes the ground crew's job immeasurably more difficult. To assist the pilot in determining wind direction right up to the last moment, the crew chief holds up a small wind sock as the pilot aims the airship toward him. Two teams of three men are assigned to catch the trailing nose lines as the blimp nears the ground. They grab the ropes and run to the side, holding the nose into the wind, while the remainder of the crew rushes in to grasp the handrail on the gondola and load shotbags aboard.

Blimps are at their most helpless during landings when crosswinds and gusts can roll them precariously. Oddly enough, though, calm days are no particular blessing, for with no wind whatsoever, the pilot's ability to control the blimp is considerably reduced as it nears the ground and loses forward speed. The ideal condition is a steady ten-mile-per-hour breeze, just enough to keep some air flowing over the rudders and elevators so that the pilot can use them effectively to control the blimp and help the struggling ground crew.

When flying operations are completed for the day, the blimp is walked to its mast by the crew, each member holding fast to the handrail or a nose line. The huge airship is inched toward the locking cup atop the mast, where another crewman waits to wrestle the hitching ball into position for locking.

The crew chief, standing in front of the mast and craning his neck upward, orchestrates this delicate series of movements with a flourish of hand signals and shouted orders. Once the blimp is locked on the mast and shut down, auxiliary blowers are placed on the two ballonet intake scoops to maintain proper envelope pressure as the restless helium cools and contracts at night. At least one crewman stays on watch after the others leave. The blimp is never left alone.

Even in repose, the blimp seems to have a life ot its own. It tracks fitfully around the mast on its wheel as the breeze eddies and shifts. Occasionally the tail lifts gracefully into the air as wind currents bubble underneath the enormous fins. Automatic pressure sensors switch on the electric ballonet blowers from time to time, puffing outside air into the two internal cells as the helium pressure falls throughout the night. Once an hour, the lone crewman on watch climbs into the car, sticks his head up into a sealed Plexiglas bubble in the roof, and shines a flashlight at the two ballonets, which look like a pair of slumbering elephants in the dark of the envelope's innards. A vertical column of numbers on each ballonet, like the Plimsoll mark on the bow of a ship, enables him to read the degree of ballonet inflation. This information, recorded twenty-four times a day and 365 days a year, is supplemented by a daily check of helium purity. Taken together, these two figures form a precise record of the envelope's aging process. About once a year, the blimp is attached to a mobile purifying machine which removes air and moisture from the helium and restores it to nearly 100 percent purity. The ballonets are inspected regularly from within. A trap door on the underside of the envelope is unzipped and a crew member climbs inside with a floodlight to check for wear. In the dark he is also able to locate holes in the skin by looking for tiny spots of sunlight showing through.

The Goodyear crews have been flying their airships for more than fifty years, so they execute their routines to perfection with ease. Although crew duties appear simple in the telling, the routine is complex in the performance of these various tasks. But mastering the techniques of one of the world's most unusual jobs offers a unique satisfaction. □

Unless the blimp is moored to its mast, these two nose lines are the best means the ground crew has to control it. The lines remain attached and trail from the nose in flight.

The day's work over, the *Columbia* lies moored to its portable mooring mast. A single crewman will watch all night, monitoring the automatic systems and staying alert for bad weather.

GOODYEAR

5

THE ROAD SHOW

The little *Mayflower* has been retired now, but this modified blimp—it has a slightly different shape—ranged from Houston, shown here, to New England.

Goodyear has this problem: there are a great many people to whom it must say "No." It hurts to say that, but the three United States–based Goodyear blimps simply cannot oblige the thousands of requests for their presence at this clambake and that county fair. The clambake and the county fair are almost certain to occur on the same day and to be hundreds of miles away from each other. Blimps are amazing machines, but they can travel at only about thirty-five miles per hour. Therefore, scheduling the three beauties occasionally means giving one event the nod and telling the other, "We'll be happy to try to fit you in next year."

The annual itinerary of each blimp is mind-boggling, an exercise in logistics and scheduling that would occupy the staff of a good-sized army. The close record kept by the company of the summer tours for the three United States–based blimps in 1976 showed that the *Mayflower* (now replaced by the larger *Enterprise*), *America*, and *Columbia* flew a total of 120,000 air miles; at thirty-five mph, that is 3,429 hours of in-transit flying, not counting the time spent on local flights at each town and event they visited. The three airships flew in twenty-eight states and touched down at eighty-three major cities during the fast-paced summer, and it is estimated that by summer's end, some sixty million people had seen a blimp firsthand.

The season during which the blimps operate away from their bases begins in the spring and lasts approximately six months. The off-season is occupied primarily with maintenance, refurbishing, and local promotional efforts. The routes the blimps are to travel are carefully planned before the season opens in order to make optimum use of available time and to arrange transit flying in a logical sequence, thereby minimizing wasted trips and backtracking.

Attendance of a blimp has become traditional at some events. For instance, there is always a blimp on station at the Indianapolis 500 Memorial Day Race, and the America's Cup yacht racing series is another must. Golf tournaments and football games also fill the calendar, and the greater the size of the potential audience, the better for Goodyear. Many stops on the tour are unrelated to public events. They are just goodwill visits meant to increase popular awareness of the Goodyear name.

Due to the operational limi-

All of Goodyear's American blimps are named after yachts that have been victorious in the America's Cup Race. Here, the *Mayflower* cruises over one of the America's Cup flotillas near Newport, Rhode Island.

tations of the blimps, certain areas of the country are out of bounds. The practical limit of the airships' flying altitude is around 3,000 feet above sea level, with an absolute maximum of 10,000 feet—so it is obvious that cities such as Denver and Albuquerque are out of luck. At those locations the blimp would be hard pressed to lift its own weight much less carry passengers or heavy television gear.

Flights between cities are usually made during daylight hours and normally average about 300 miles, which translates into some eight hours of flying. Two pilots share the flying duty, alternating in the captain's chair on the left side every hour. The off-duty pilots travel with the ground crew in a rolling circus of vehicles that includes a bus, a small van, and a huge trailer-truck with generators, spare parts, and machinery. Tagging along in this gypsy train are the private cars belonging to the families of crew members. As many as twenty-two Goodyear employees may travel with a blimp, including five pilots, seventeen crewmen, and a public relations representative.

These treks that attend any intercity movement of a blimp have a kind of riotous organization to them. The public

A huge trailer truck (far left) leads the caravan; the navigator in the right seat does map duty. The crew bus (top) has an office, and a complete machine shop (bottom) is built into the trailer.

The ground crew precedes the blimp's arrival, and rigging the mast resembles the setup of a circus. The mast must be in place before the airship's arrival.

relations representative generally precedes the group by a couple of days, acting as an advance man. The senior pilot is responsible for ground navigation. He has the unenviable duty of leading the main group while reading a map, often in the shotgun seat of the big semi rig, the slowest single vehicle and therefore the logical choice as pace setter.

The navigator is under constant pressure all the way. He dare not: (1) get lost; (2) drive in such a way as to break up the caravan; or (3) miss meeting the blimp at its destination. The blimp simply cannot land without its crew. Of course, no navigator is perfect, and there is more than one horror story of part of the convoy barreling down the interstate, watching in appalled fascination as the other portion passes going in the opposite direction.

Strange things can happen along the convoy's route—and often do. One Goodyear vehicle with the old yellow paint job (the color scheme is now blue-and-white) was plagued by people who climbed into it at stoplights on the assumption that it was a taxicab. On another occasion, the pilots in the blimp tried to be helpful by directing the ground navigator along what looked like a shortcut to the airport. Things went swimmingly until the truck driver found himself having to back away from a low underpass that the pilots had failed to notice. The result was a two-hour traffic jam, naturally at the height of the rush hour. It did little to enhance Goodyear's public image. Since then, the blimp's pilots have left the driving to the drivers.

Usually, it is not difficult for the ground procession to match or even exceed the airship's moderate cross-country progress. After a morning takeoff, there is plenty of time to disassemble the mooring site, clean up, settle airport bills, hit the road, stop for lunch, and still make it to the next mooring site before the blimp gets there.

The airship and the ground convoy are in regular radio contact with each other, so there are few surprises. Upon arriving at the destination aerodrome, the crew immediately begins erecting the mooring mast. The mast is made of three sections, fitted together end-to-end, then raised like a tent pole and

Although the ground crew's work may not be the most glamorous part of blimp operations, the Goodyear crews have always had lots of willing applicants— and even some volunteers!

GOODYEAR
N4A
GOODYEAR
GOODYEAR
GOODYEAR
GOODYEAR

guyed by staking cables.

When the blimp looms up over the horizon, an unspoken message always seems to sweep through the streets. Although nobody deliberately signals the citizenry, the folks always somehow know the blimp is about to land in their town. And when that town is a small one like Tifton, Georgia, or Zanesville, Ohio, the arrival is a major event.

By the time the blimp is on its final approach, gaggles of wide-mouthed, wide-eyed children and adults are elbow-to-elbow at the airport fence, mesmerized by the sights unfolding before them. Various "experts" can be heard murmuring completely erroneous information to gullible children. But neither truth nor numbers matter. It is the experience that counts. For years, these people will talk about the day the blimp came to town.

In bigger cities, the crowd is every bit as large, every bit as susceptible. "Are they landing it?" "Are they letting it down?" "Yeah, I think so. There, see? See those ropes? That's the landing gear. They'll tie it down with those." There are a thousand explanations for the blimp's every move; the strangeness of it all compels people to say *something*, anything, even conjuring up a fantasy or two.

Once the blimp is moored, the awestruck crowd soon finds a way to approach it. It is an unwritten law of human nature. The blimp is here, therefore the people will come unto it. The crew fends off the most aggressive of the crowd in a friendly way, making certain that curiosity causes harm to neither person nor blimp.

Eventually, the crew climbs on their bus and heads for a motel near the airport, leaving one crew member to stand the night's first watch. He can call on the off-duty crew in the event of a weather emergency. Long after the summer night's dark has settled, though, he will still be handing out pamphlets and answering questions with whatever energy he has left. Finally, the last youngster borne on the shoulders of the last adult will run out of things to ask, and the crewman will turn to other duties—monitoring pressure, working on some equipment, keeping an ever-wary eye on the weather.

A blimp's typical working day: flying Goodyear customers on short hops, an air show, or a TV camera mission. Then the crew packs it all up to drive to the next town and do it again.

If the blimp has planned a stay of several days, passenger flights will be the main order of business. Rides on the Goodyear blimps are offered by company invitation only, with Goodyear's district management office controlling the seat allotment. Most of the lucky riders are customers of Goodyear's various retail divisions or local dignitaries and members of the press. Despite the airship's huge size, the small car can handle only six passengers plus the pilot—a surprise to those with visions of transoceanic zeppelin travel dancing in their heads. The ride is usually a thirty-minute spin over the town and back, the pilot occasionally plunking a delighted passenger into the left seat for a try at handling the airship. After the flight, the blimp returns to the airport and quickly exchanges its guests for another group while the ground crew hangs onto the handrails and nose lines. The ship is seldom on the ground for more than a minute between flights. After a load of passengers has disembarked, they receive small namecards signed by the pilot as mementos of their flight.

On evenings when the blimp is assigned to fly a night-sign mission, the routine changes. The Super Skytacular night sign has its own set of equipment that must be installed and checked before the flight begins. Mounted on the flank of each blimp are thousands of lights (actually automotive taillight bulbs about the size of flashlight bulbs, covered with plastic discs colored red, yellow, green, and blue), which enable it to produce the images and words of the animated night-sign messages. Although the lights are permanently affixed, the mechanism that reads the computer-programmed tapes must be installed for a night-sign flight; due to its weight, it must be removed afterward. Out come the passenger seats and in goes the tape reader, along with an externally mounted auxiliary turbine power unit to generate the additional electricity the lights require. This Garrett AiResearch generator is similar to the type used for ground power and air-conditioning on airplanes.

The night sign is an electronic marvel. In the early days, a blimp was wired to display only a single message at a time, and it had to be rewired each time that message was altered. Today's signs are computer-controlled super-whiz contrivances that produce the most complex images and effects of any light sign in the world. A computer at Goodyear Aerospace's Akron facility is programmed to allow a technician to design a message (in English or any other language: the *Europa* has "spoken" eight languages so far) and record it on magnetic tape. The completed cassette is checked for correctness and then dispatched to each blimp for use. A trained technician goes aloft and operates a machine that can read the tape and illuminate each one of the thousands of bulbs in precisely the correct sequence and for

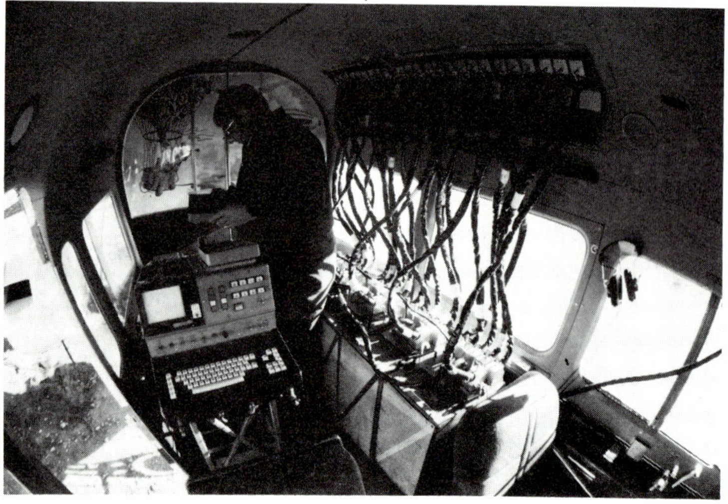

Readying a night sign flight: attaching the generator (top left), checking computer-programmed light sequences (top right), and setting up the onboard computer (bottom), which reads the tape and lights each bulb at the proper moment.

The night sign's automotive taillight bulbs are permanently attached to the envelope's exterior. The four colors—red, green, yellow, and blue—can be combined to form other colors.

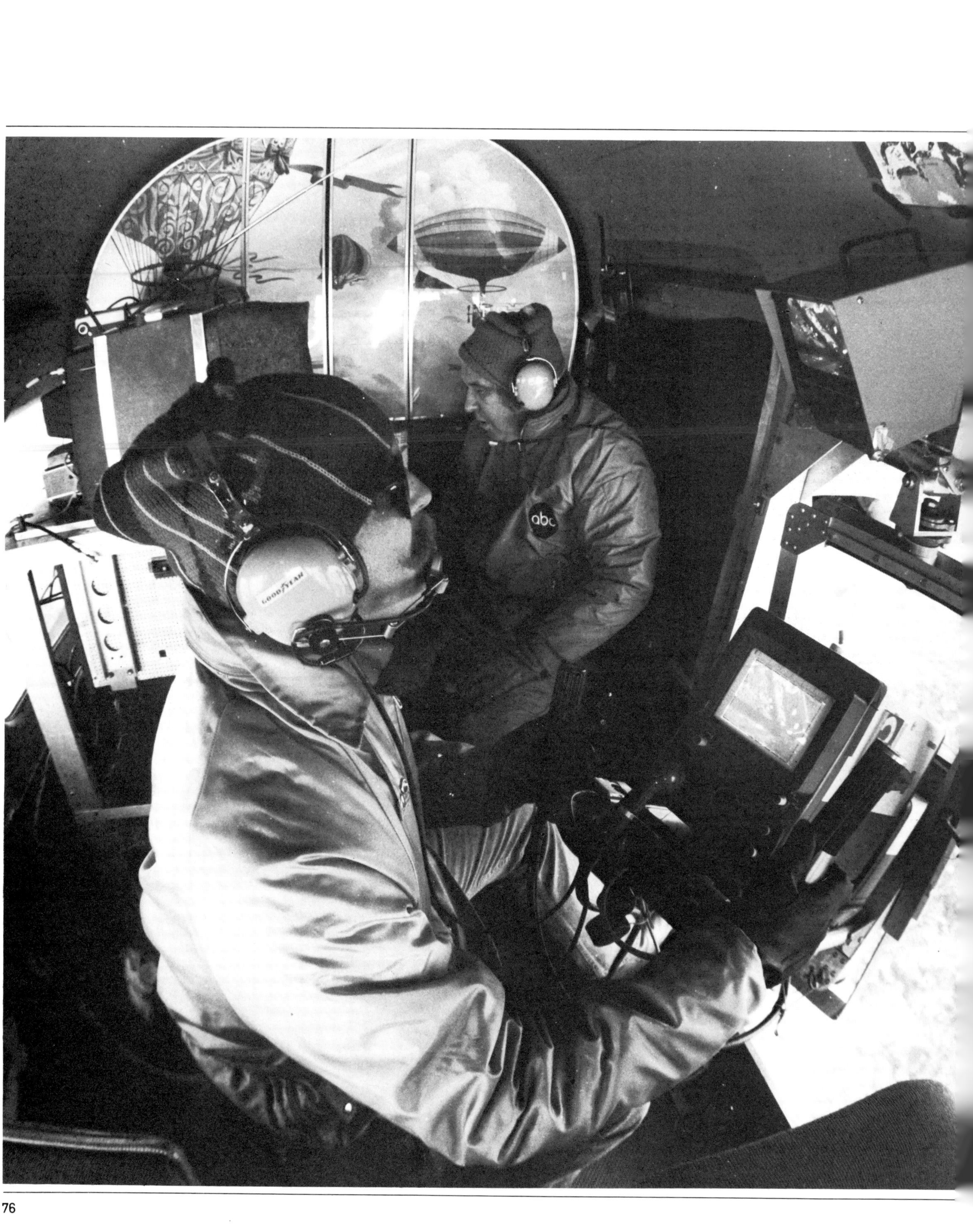
abc

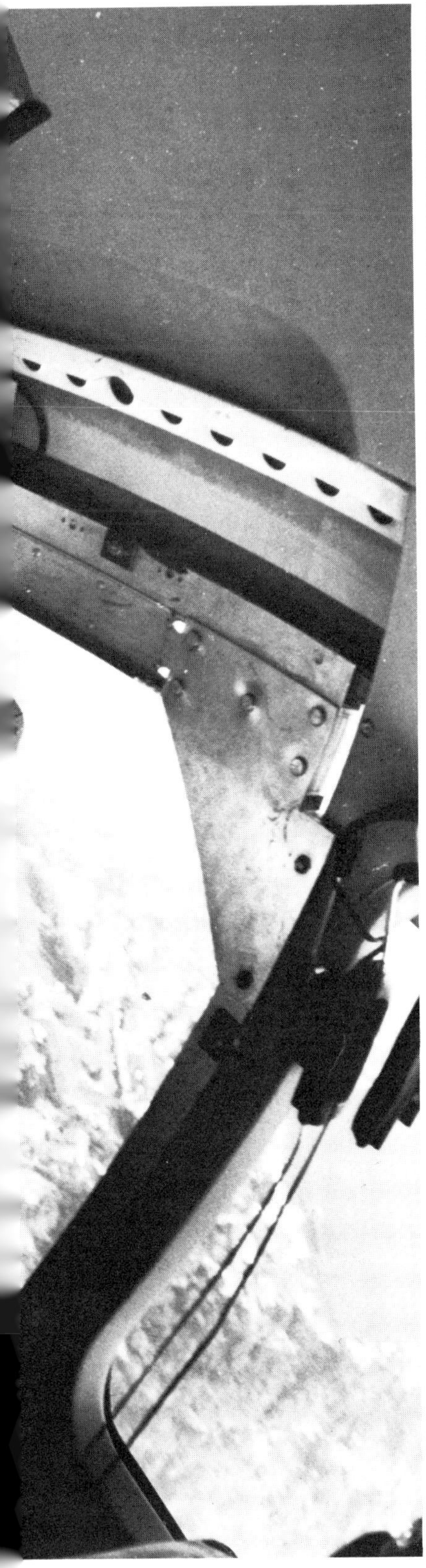

the proper length of time.

When the sign first lights up at night, there is occasionally a concurrent light show at the switchboard of the local police station as people unfamiliar with the night sign phone in their alarms. To try to minimize this, one tape begins with the message: "IT'S NO UFO—JUST THE GOODYEAR BLIMP!"

Although the night signs are used to promote many Goodyear products, most of the programming is of a public-service nature. Non-profit events and charities are mentioned on the sign, between dazzling four-color designs and even animated cartoons. A typewriter keyboard makes up part of the night-sign installation, and the technician can use it to spell out messages directly onto the sign instead of playing the tape. For the past several years, the *Europa* has flown all night over the twenty-four-hour auto race at LeMans, using its sign to broadcast position reports on cars vying for the lead.

Another traditional role for the blimp stems from its marvelous ability to serve as a camera platform for photography or for television broadcasting. Goodyear makes arrangements with the television networks to provide the blimp for aerial coverage of public events. The company also supplies a lightweight color camera and onboard electronics, all specially modified for use in the blimp. The network or station need send only a cameraman and video technician. A microwave transmitter sends the camera's signal from the blimp to a dish antenna and receiver on the ground. This signal can be fed live into the network or put on videotape for later broadcast or replay. The television crewmen stay in constant contact with their director by means of a separate two-way radio link, to which the pilots also listen for positioning cues.

Different sports events require varying camera and piloting techniques. The low drone of the blimp's engines has been known to irritate golfers and tennis players and, as a result, the standard operating procedure at Forest Hills or Pebble Beach is to keep well off to the side and let the camera's enormous Schneider 30:1 zoom lens close the gap. Football players and fans do not worry much about noise, however, so they see the blimp almost directly overhead. During coverage of a motorcycle race in California, one airborne cameraman took a lambasting from the director for failing to keep his camera trained on the leaders of the race. The man on the camera was not at fault, though; a stiff wind was blowing, and the blimp was moving backward even with the throttles open wide.

Goodyear provides the airship and camera with its giant zoom lens; the TV network provides a cameraman and video technician. In return, the blimp and its pilot get a plug on the air.

The blimp *Europa*, though registered in the U.S. (the *N* prefix on the tail tells you that), carries the Goodyear name throughout Western Europe. There are no sporting events in Rome's Colosseum, but *Europa* has an audience anyway.

The Goodyear blimps have appeared in a number of Hollywood motion pictures, with roles in *Nashville, Once Is Not Enough, Two-Minute Warning, A Star Is Born,* and the Beatles' film *Help!,* among others. A blimp never enjoyed a starring role, however, until one was featured in Paramount's film version of the novel *Black Sunday*. The plot centers around a terrorist scheme to commandeer a blimp and use it to carry a large bomb over the Super Bowl game. Three blimps were used during the filming of various action sequences, and many of the blimp crew members and pilots appear in the film as well.

Goodyear also makes its airships available for a variety of scientific purposes. One was used as a flying wind tunnel in some aerodynamic studies. By hanging test vehicles below the blimp, scientists were able to obtain accurate airflow data, unencumbered by the confusing side effects that may have been caused by the walls of the usual static wind tunnel. Another blimp was a target for sonic-boom experiments at Edwards Air Force Base in California. It hovered at 2,000 feet while jets flew past at supersonic speeds, aiming shock waves at measuring instruments on the airship. Pollution-monitoring equipment has often been carried aloft aboard the *Columbia* over Los Angeles, and the same airship has been used for urban-planning surveys and transportation studies.

One of the most fascinating, and oddly appropriate, uses to which the *Columbia* was put was in assisting the American Cetacean Society in its annual count of the California gray whale, which migrates along the Pacific coast close to shore. These whale-watch flights, which took place through the 1970's, were flown at a low and lazy four knots—about the same speed as the cruising whales but certainly far slower than any airplane could fly. These flights began to show in the late 1970s that the animals have staged what may be a comeback from their once diminishing numbers. In fact, recent indications are that other whale species are inhabiting the coastal waters in greater numbers, possibly to seek refuge from the slaughter that continues in the open ocean.

After more than four decades of successful commercial airship operations all over America, Goodyear began in 1971 to assemble components for a fourth blimp that would operate in Europe, in the hope that it would generate the same kind of excitement as that produced by the United States fleet. In many ways, the European venture would have to differ from the operation in the United States. The many national boundaries to be crossed, for example, and the red tape that would attend each crossing could make life infinitely more complex for a European crew. The countries of western Europe are not very large in terms of area, and distances between them are short, but the bureaucratic boundaries can stretch the kilometers.

Language was bound to be another problem, as would the innumerable filings and permissions that must accompany almost every private and cor-

The parade of Kentucky Derby hopefuls at Churchill Downs is nearly lost in the ocean of human hopefuls there to bet on their favorites.

porate flight in European airspace. And in Europe, everything would certainly cost more.

First, a hangar for the ship had to be constructed. In Capena, Italy, for $2.5 million, Goodyear built a modern and completely equipped facility capable of servicing any need. While the Italian hangar was being readied, the components of the *Europa* were shipped to Cardington, England, for assembly at an airship hangar still maintained there by the Royal Aircraft Establishment. When the new *Europa* took off from the Cardington base, it was the first time an airship had flown over England in more than forty years. After being test-flown, the *Europa* prepared to cross the Channel for its first tour of the Continent.

The crewmen of the *Europa* represent a variety of nationalities, ten countries in all. From the start, the intention was for the American team that led the initial *Europa* crew to be slowly replaced until the crew was made up entirely of native Europeans.

Most of the original European crew members had spent part of a tour season with one of the American airships before going to work in Europe, so they knew the basics of blimping from actual experience rather than from theory.

With the passage of time, the operation in Europe has become much smoother, as the various governments and their agencies have become used to the comings and goings of the *Europa*. The interminable border delays that marred the first tours—crewmen and customs officials haggling over such fine points as whether or not the arrival of an airship constituted the importation of helium—have dissolved as crossings have become routine. Traffic controllers, bewildered at first by the bizarre craft that tracked across their radar screens at a crawl, now welcome the *Europa* into their airspace. To date, the ship has flown in fourteen countries.

Europe has also served as the staging locale for the first airships to be produced as rivals to Goodyear's fleet. In West Germany and England, blimps are being built or are operating for commercial firms who have every hope of showing a profit. The Goodyear airships are no longer the only commercial blimps in the skies, and for airship fans that is good news. □

The Super Skytacular night sign can provide animation, moving-word messages, or it can just plain show off, as it does here with a geometric pattern of all four colors.

GOODYEAR

6
AMERICA'S SWEET-HEARTS

Not something you see every day: the blimp makes friends at sea with delighted pleasure-boaters on Long Island Sound.

Every few years an expert appears to proclaim the rebirth of airships. Most of these people tell anyone in the newspaper or television industry who will listen that airships are not irrelevant artifacts of the past but the heralds of a future age when humankind will again turn to the efficient airship for transport, that the old zeppelins were too far ahead of their time, and that their ascendancy has come.

These stirrings of interest, nearly carbon copies of one another, seem as regular and inevitable as elections and taxes. They usually generate a flurry of excitement among lighter-than-air proponents and a few others who are hearing it for the first time.

The rest, having heard it all before, respond by flatly panning the airship and anyone crazy enough to suggest that it could replace anything flying today. Having done so, they put their responses back in the file cabinets and await the next cycle.

Goodyear alone among the parties to this seasonal debate stays quietly aloof, for it alone knows the truth. To argue whether the blimp is efficient or vulnerable to the weather or cost-effective or profitable is simply to miss the point.

The secret, which the blimps hold within their ethereal hulls, is that they embody some spirit, some quality that sets them apart from ordinary experience and that draws people to them. The people who serve on the Goodyear crews understand this perhaps better than anyone else, for they willingly abandon any semblance of a normal life when they sign on. Although each individual

Master modeler Edward Chavez exhibits his highly detailed scale model of the *Columbia* on display at the Smithsonian National Air & Space Museum.

may choose different words to describe what happens, all are saying essentially the same thing: they are hooked. They fly blimps because they have to. No substitute will do.

Goodyear has no particular desire to construct blimps for a waiting world. Its airships are not for sale (though many were chartered by other companies in the earlier days of blimp operations). Goodyear does not measure the success of its fleet of four in terms of profit or loss, pounds of freight lifted, or distance covered. The blimps exist simply to persuade people to feel kindly toward Goodyear, and, as a recognizable image, the blimps have been unbeatable. A corporation the size of Goodyear does nothing by chance, so studies are made periodically to assess the public sentiment toward the great silver gasbags. Results are not merely positive, they are almost hysterically favorable.

Because the blimps tend to generate so much emotion and excitement, and also because so few people are actually familiar with how they work, strange things often happen to the airships and their crews.

One elderly passenger was surprised by the large wheel at the captain's right hand. This wheel controls the elevators that direct the ship up and down, but nobody had explained that to her. When she demanded to be let off before the blimp had even departed, the crew asked why. "I'm not flying with any pilot who's in a wheelchair," was her answer.

Most VIPs are very gracious and enjoy the ride when it is offered. Richard Petty, the NASCAR racing champion and user of Goodyear's racing tires, spent the first few moments of his flight searching for his seat belt before he was told he did not need one. (The Goodyear blimps are the only certified powered aircraft that do not require seat belts aboard.) Dwight D. Eisenhower is reported to have dropped what he was doing at the approach of a blimp, accepting with a child's enthusiasm the crew's invitation for a ride. A week later, the crew received a note of thanks from the former president, a new convert to lighter-than-air.

Other big shots have been less pleasant. Passenger flights for Goodyear's friends are very tightly scheduled in order to minimize time and handling on the ground. Passengers are asked to be at the airport well ahead of their scheduled takeoff because it is undesirable to have the blimp tarrying in the grip of the ground crew. The crew does not like it, and neither does the blimp. A well-known United States senator was invited for a ride with his grandson, but they arrived late. As the disappointed boy watched the departing blimp grow smaller in the distance, his famous grandfather tried to bring the weight of his office to bear on the crew. Like any grandparent, the senator was loathe to face an unhappy child, and the crew's explanations about

on-time operations got nowhere.

"That's all well and good," thundered the senator, "but *you* explain to the boy why he can't have a blimp ride."

One of the blimp pilots looked at the boy, smiled, and said simply, "I'm sorry, but you won't be able to have a ride in the blimp because your grandfather was late."

In 1968, the blimp covering the Sebring twelve-hour race in Florida was diverted from its television role to assist law-enforcement officials in rounding up a fugitive. The fleeing felon was ultimately spotted running through the woods. One can only imagine what went through his mind when he looked up and saw what was making all that racket overhead. Explaining his capture-by-blimp to his cellmates must have been even worse.

At the same auto race, the Goodyear Racing Division staff was worried about the impending weather. "Why not check with the blimp crew? They're weather experts, they have to be," someone suggested. So the tire engineers asked the blimpos to watch the weather, and for twenty-four hours they observed, measured, discussed, and evaluated. The decision: rain, and lots of it. Definitely. No question about it. The racing division's tire-busters went to work, mounting rain tires for all their customers. When the race was run, it turned out to be the warmest and sunniest day ever. Not a drop of rain.

Then there are all those crazy schemes people keep coming up with. One millionaire wanted to hire a blimp to hoist his yacht out of a landlocked lake and drop it into the Gulf of Mexico. Another fellow, explaining he was an advertising executive from the West Coast, phoned to say he wanted to buy an airship so that he could paint it to look like a pineapple. He also wanted to rent one of Goodyear's hangars and paint it to look like a pineapple can. His plan: to photograph the blimp/pineapple flying in and out of the can. No one can accuse him of not thinking big.

The blimp crew sometimes has to fight its own popularity. For example, one of the crews arrived at their assigned motel only to find a note tacked to the office door: "Back at 6 o'clock. Gone to the airport to see blimp."

Nude bathers at Black's Beach in La Jolla, California, complained not about prying eyes from the blimp's passing gondola but about the huge shadow it cast. They claimed that until the blimp passed and the sun came back out, they froze half to death.

Two nuns once swore they saw a blimp land inside a football stadium, something no blimp has ever done. A woman insisted to authorities that a blimp had landed in her garden and disturbed her plants. And a man once called the police to report that the blimp had just flown down his street and knocked down all the television antennas. Whatever it was he saw, it was not a blimp.

Lightplanes are drawn to a blimp like moths to a lightbulb. They circle endlessly, sometimes to take pictures, sometimes just for fun. They waggle their wings, wave through windows, shine flashlights—anything and everything. Of course, the sheer size of the blimp makes it difficult to judge how far away

Air show fans (facing page) at Abbotsford, British Columbia, find relief from the heat in the blimp's big shadow. Some Goodyear guests take a brief ride (top), while fence hangers in Newport, Rhode Island, watch a takeoff (bottom).

On approach to a landing at a remote field (left), the *Columbia* shows why blimps need plenty of room to operate. But the response on the ground (facing page) makes this blimp operation worth the effort.

it is, so most lightplane pilots think they are much closer than they actually are. The blimp is also a lot nimbler than many pilots believe, and it can turn more tightly than almost any airplane ever built, a fact that surprises many of the pilots who buzz the blimp with vague notions of outmaneuvering the big bag.

Air-traffic controllers are apparently so jarred by encountering such a strange object that they lose their crisp, businesslike staccato and start "aw-geeing" like kids, gushing questions about speed and range, requesting rides for themselves and their families. It is not unusual for a slow-moving blimp to be used by the tower as a reporting point for incoming aircraft (as in "Bonanza nine-three victor, report abeam the blimp on down wind." "Uh . . . this is nine-three victor, could you say again, please?")

One day when the *Columbia* was headed inland for Arizona, it began to approach its pressure altitude, the height above sea level beyond which it cannot rise without valving helium. The pilot determined that the airship would clear the pass in the mountains on the course ahead, but not by much. The *Columbia* nudged into the pass less than 100 feet above the pavement of an interstate highway just as a long-haul trucker topped the grade coming in the opposite direction. Nobody on the crew has yet found the words to describe the expression on the driver's face when the whole scene finally registered. They do remember that he parked on the shoulder for a very long time.

On an approach to an Oregon airport in a thick fog, the *Columbia* was proceeding over the water to an instrument landing. Suddenly, out of the gloom, the pilot spotted a fishing boat below. He threw the props into reverse and howled to a halt, opened the window, and asked the fishermen on the deck below, "Which way to Mexico?" Every one of them pointed dead south, mouths open, knees limp.

The blimp and its crew are blessed with freedom from the humdrum. Sometimes that freedom is a mixed blessing—but there are times when the job is an unalloyed privilege. One such occasion was the flight with a five-year-old leukemia victim whose prognosis was as bad as a prognosis can be. Frank Hogan, then chief pilot for the airship *America*, put the little girl at the controls and helped her direct the big blimp.

"Grandma, I *drove* it," the little girl squealed.

Some time later, someone asked her what her greatest thrill had been. There was not a moment's hesitation. "The balloon," she said. She could not know, of course, but almost everyone who has shared the experience would agree. □

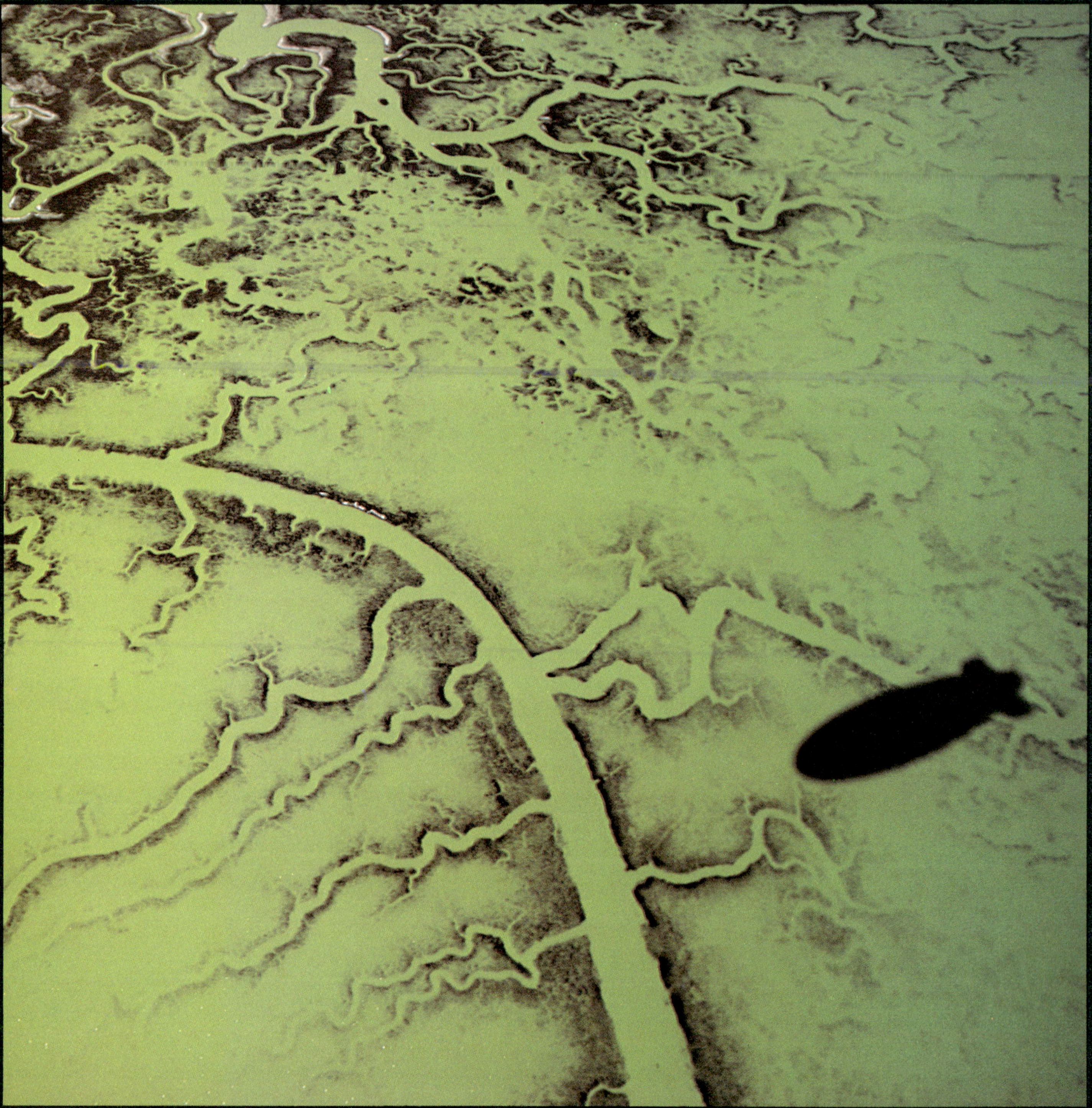

7
SAILING LOW

Minitrucks just off the boat in Savannah, Georgia, line up in ribbons of color. Viewed from the blimp, the shapes of the individual trucks become subordinate to the orderly pattern they form.

One of the ironies of aviation is that as aircraft have gained speed they have reached upward toward higher altitudes, so that the faster they fly, the higher they fly. To the pilot or passenger, however, it is as if no change had occurred. If you look out the window at 100 miles per hour from a few hundred feet above the ground or at Mach 2 and six miles up, the earth's quilt seems to roll past at about the same speed in either case. Jet transports may have shortened the travel time between cities that were once far apart, but by climbing into the stratosphere in order to do it, they have virtually removed the passenger from the most intimate sensations of travel.

Airships need the densest air, the kind you can find only close to the surface of the earth near sea level. To lift a payload with any sort of efficiency, the blimp must limit itself to the lowest regions of the atmosphere. The jet airliner climbs into a near-vacuum in order to reduce the amount of friction as air rubs against its skin and to escape the worst of the weather. The blimp seeks instead the confines of the troposphere, where the weight of the tightly packed atmospheric gases buoys the lighter helium in the envelope. It is here that the air roils with weather: winds, ice, lightning —forces beyond the imagination and far mightier than the airship. Yet the airship must survive here, and it does.

In a way, blimps ought to be considered surface transports, except that they fly just above the surface. The lucky airship passenger enjoys the vista of the railroad or automobile traveler, only from a slightly higher vantage that allows one to see just over that next hill. People who fly cross-country for the first time in a blimp invariably remark on the richness of detail in the earth below. It is almost more than the mind can take in at once. From the window of a blimp, you can make out not only individual people on the ground, but even their facial expressions (normal: mouth open, eyes wide) as they stare back at you.

A California citrus grove imposes its mosaic upon the subtler patterns of stone and soil. Humans like to tend an orderly field.

You are a visitor in backyards and city streets, in schoolyards and farmers' markets, and the entire panoply seems only just out of reach. A soft spring forest, with its brilliant green of new leaves, billows under your imagined outstretched fingertips like the most luxurious velvet; the touch of it might be like that of moss. From this moment forth, one thing is certain: whenever you are near a forest, you will always remember this view.

When we look down on our world from very close above it, this perspective changes more than the way we see. It alters our ideas as well. For the first time, we begin to perceive a community, a planet, a context within which our humanness takes on new meaning. The difference between our view of things from inside our little dwellings and that from aloft — where we see our own dwelling place as one of hundreds, thousands, millions — is so great a cognitive leap that the experience leaves us profoundly grateful.

The blimp flies in a most archaic manner—low and slow —but from it, we relearn why the old dirigibles had huge windows for their passengers' view of the vista below. We begin to comprehend why that view was so hypnotic, why long, silent minutes of transfixion would grow into hours of mesmerized fascination. The blimp reminds us why humankind dreamed of flying in the first place: not merely to get from Seattle to Dallas in three and a half hours, though that certainly has its place; the reason, it turns out, for that pressing urge to fly was to see what it looks like from up there and, having seen, to understand.

The Indiana farm country, bathed in golden afternoon sun, shows off nature's rich autumn textures of corduroy squares joined by tree-lined seams.

Scatter rugs of logs on the Fraser River's mirror surface form log booms that are a common sight in Vancouver—but an uncommon sight from a blimp.

The blimp's buoyant cousin, the hot-air balloon, floats serenely over farmland, its colorful canopy like a giant flower bud that has sprouted from the vegetation below.

La Guardia Airport, New York City: glinty, sharp-edged machines gather like suckling babes at their mothers' breasts, while nearby, steel-gray organs and arteries are nourished by commercial blood.

An irrigation system creates a water ballet of spray that might be choreographed to suit a theme from The *Nutcracker*.

In the Amish country near Lancaster, Pennsylvania, two buggy-borne observers peek out—and up—from their centuries-old form of land transport.

Try to find the faces that are *not* looking at the camera. When the *America* made a low pass near a Connecticut beach, it captured the attention of most—but not quite all—sunbathers.

Like a digital computer made real, this railroad yard viewed from above resembles a network of wires carrying color-coded packets of data.

Humankind finds its way to the most remote regions of the planet, plants a flag, and builds.

Kelp filaments borne by the currents scurry through some shallows along the Pacific coast. This watery forest is the grazing land for the fragile sea life that thrives in shallows.

Rowboats for rent at a peaceful park pond huddle together like fallen leaves caught in the eddy of a brook.

When technology spawns a community, the result often looks very much like this airborne view of Daly City, in California.

Prime farmland?—no, these are actually the salt ponds of San Francisco Bay. The mineral content of the water gives them their terra-cotta coloring.

This grownup's sand-box with its mechanized toys is rendered into a scallop shell by the tracks of bulldozers that tire-lessly rearrange it.

Plastic film used to cut water loss in this field of freshly planted crops lends an eerie sheen to the scene, transforming this aerial view of a huge field into the micro-image of a computer chip.

FUTURE-
BLIMP

It is very unlikely that airships will make a comeback on the scale of the great zeppelin airlines, but that does not mean there is no future at all for the blimp. In fact, the prospects for airships have not been better in a long time. Part of the problem has been that the people who love the blimps want to see them take over *everything:* passenger carrying, fish-spotting, crop-dusting—you name it. The most serious proponents of airships for future commercial use are bothered by this "giggle factor," the all-encompassing affection for blimps that will not listen to reason. Even the most modern blimp would fail if it were put up against an equally modern jet and forced to compete along the same routes. Most people today travel because they are going somewhere. The less time it takes, the better. (If you need a demonstration to convince you of that, watch closely the next time your jumbo-jet captain announces the Grand Canyon on the public address system. Never mind that he is talking to the ten percent of the passengers who are lucky enough to be sitting next to windows with a view of it; the rest of his audience is more interested in the movie.)

If airships are to make a place for themselves in the future, they must first demonstrate to everyone concerned with building and buying them that they will operate profitably. Airships can operate profitably, but only at certain very specific jobs and only in certain very special places. Ask yourself what Chile, Canada, and Brazil have in common—they are all nations that have a great deal of interest in airships for the future—and you will begin to understand where and how blimps succeed best in today's world.

Short-haul, heavy-lift. Say that ten times, and it is yours for life. Short-haul, heavy-lift describes the sort of mission at which modern airships can succeed best in modern commercial application, and most serious airship projects are aimed at exactly that market. Airships can succeed by doing something very well that no other device can match for performance, and that something involves moving very heavy, very large objects over fairly short distances. If you match that ability to a remote area that lacks a well-developed rail and road system, the airship wins hands down. Thus, various countries that are interested in developing large-scale construction and energy projects in areas that are inaccessible to conventional lifting machines are beginning to look quite seriously at the lifting ability of a blimplike machine that uses modern design and technology. Although such a future airship would sport some very up-to-date features, the basic principle and even the materials used to build it would remain unchanged from traditional blimp construction.

Probably the greatest drawback to airships that were built in the past is not any severe vulnerability to weather. Even jet airplanes have learned to avoid phenomena such as thunderstorms and wind shear, so in that respect, blimps and airplanes are virtually equal. The navy blimps of the 1960s demonstrated conclusively that airships can stand up to pretty bad storms. No, the single greatest moment of vulnerability for a blimp is its approach and landing. It becomes much less controllable at very low airspeeds when there is less air moving over its control surfaces and therefore less force for the pilot to use in changing direction. Traditional blimps have also required throngs of ground crew, who were needed just for the simple act of snaring the airship and mooring it. In difficult winds, that job can be like trying to wrestle with a whale.

Although airship designers argue over the best way to solve this problem, it does appear to be solvable, which is good news. One approach would be to design blimps with a sort of wing shape that would make them more like airplanes, so that they would land and take off in a similar way but using only short runways. This design would ensure that there was always plenty of air moving over the control surfaces, but still the question of an airship's ability to *hover* would be left open.

Helicopters hover very nicely; that is, they are able to remain aloft and maintain position very precisely with respect to the ground, even when a fairly stiff wind is blowing. For picking up and dropping off cargo as well as for landing operations with only one or two ground-crew members to help, a future airship should be able to hover. The answer to hoverability is *vectored thrust,* which is a fancy way of saying that the airship's engines could be pointed in any desired direction and their propellers reversed when needed so that the thrust could be redirected and used to keep the blimp stationary.

Obviously, in gusty winds, a blimp pilot would really have his or her hands full even with vectored thrust because the task of hovering any aircraft is not an easy one to accomplish manually. That is where modern electronics come in. If most drawings of future blimps look disappointingly similar to the airships of the past, it is because the biggest difference in the two would be that the future version will have a flight-control system so advanced that it will almost automate the act of flying as well as greatly aid the pilot in hovering when necessary. Even ballonet operation could be made automatic thanks to the tremendous power of digital computers. Blimp designers already are working on the logic that probably would be required to produce the computer program for a blimp flight-control system. The two most advanced ideas for modern blimps—vectored thrust and electronic flight control—are not apparent when you look at illustrations of ideas for future airships, but they are still the most important new elements.

Future blimps might make use of some fibers that have been developed since the 1960s: very strong but lightweight materials such as aramid, for example. An envelope made of rubberized aramid would be stronger for equal weight compared with an envelope made with some of the older synthetics; or it might be made lighter in weight at equivalent strength. An aramid envelope would almost certainly be more expensive, too, and although its advantages might make the extra cost worthwhile, that extra cost is still too great an economic burden in today's market to justify the use of new materials.

While there are many competing designs for modern airships, many of them practical and producible, ideas alone seem to be insufficient for winning the battle when it comes to airships. Very large airship projects are enormous, multimillion-dollar investments on the part of the customers, the operators, and the airship manufacturer. For that simple reason, the most likely players in any future revival of a modern blimp for commercial application are the very largest corporations—mining and metals industries, energy companies—and governments contemplating large-scale development projects, in such areas as Canada's Northwest and the province of Alberta. Alberta lacks a transportation network and suffers from severe seasonal changes that inhibit ordinary construction and development methods. Brazil has a more moderate climate but a vast, undeveloped interior, which it would like to exploit for its resources. A modern airship would have applications in lifting heavy construction equipment directly to a site, in large-scale forestry development, where it would act as an overhead crane to lift and move felled timber, and finally, in transporting heavy and bulky parts of structures for assembly on site in minimum time. While studies have shown that airships will work well in such missions, no single party has yet stepped forward with the money and the will to undertake the development of new airships. Although the blimp of the future is not so different from the blimp of the past, building one, especially the first one, will require an enormous capital investment, and that tends to urge most potential customers to adopt a wait-and-see attitude. Inevitably, someone will be first, and then there may well be a rush to order follow-on airships.

For those who so fervently

wish for an airship revival, the scale of the projects just described is daunting. But there may be another answer for them: think small.

The truth is that although Goodyear has been the only consistent operator of blimps over the years since the United States Navy ceased its lighter-than-air flying, the activity by independent blimp boosters seeking small-scale use of airships, generally as advertising platforms, has never ceased. After all, the incredible success of the Goodyear blimps has not been lost on these people, and they simply want to capitalize on the idea.

Anheuser-Busch, a brewery based in St. Louis, Missouri, has successfully operated a pair of advertising blimps that use hot air as their buoyant medium. The two "Good Beer" blimps are smaller and simpler than the Goodyear public relations blimps, but they perform a similar function, keeping the brewery's products in the public eye at various events that draw large crowds. Because they use hot air instead of helium, they are inflated prior to each flight and then vented and repacked into their traveling trailers when the flying is over, moving from place to place on the ground.

Of course, Anheuser-Busch is a pretty big company and is able to support an airship program. What is surprising is the willingness of small, independent groups to invest their money in small-scale helium-filled blimps with the hope of selling advertising space. Many of these groups have limited budgets, and their airships are built up of older envelopes bought from storage or modified balloons from military surplus. The results of these projects have been, well . . . mixed. It is a difficult lesson to learn for the people who try to start from scratch, but the fact is that operating an airship is not easy.

In 1980, a company in New York acquired a retired blimp envelope and attempted to build an airship for advertising. The lighter-than-air circle is a tightly knit one, and the news of the project spread fast, as did rumors about the airship and the envelope it would use. Spare blimp envelopes are very scarce commodities, and insiders know where most of them are and what sort of shape they are in. When the Jordache company, a manufacturer of fashion jeans, announced that it had hired this blimp as a flying advertisement, that the blimp would be inflated at Lakehurst, New Jersey, and then flown to New York City for a spectacular introductory party, some knowledgeable airshipmen said the project would not succeed. It did not. The Jordache blimp had control problems only shortly after takeoff and struck a tree before deflating and putting an end to the big party.

Somehow, the difficulties of others have never deterred the formation of new companies almost annually with the expressed purpose of building an airship operation. Typical of the charm, dedication, and all-around entrepreneurial fervor that characterizes these tiny organizations is a company formed in Texas in 1980 called U.S. Airships, Inc. Three Texas oilmen named Tony Howard, Fred McCoun, and Bill Coleman, all of whom honestly admit to knowing n
thing about blimps
their company in th
Teaselville, near Tyl
sole promise of one
used Australian bl
had come to naught.

As the story go
Australian businessm
must have had t
blimpy visions da
their heads that curre
merize these Texa
a blimp to advertise
of cigarettes Down U
its first flight, thin
swimmingly, and t
even made an ap
on television—which
brought the house do
owners. It turns out
illegal to advertis
rettes on Australia
sion, and before long
pany was bankrupt,
a nearly new blimp
And that's where o
friends from Texas co

Bill Coleman own
air balloon wit
Tony Howard, and w
man heard about t
in Australia, he bo
blimp. That was in
since that time, he h
Fred McCoun to b
nancial manager, a
Stefan, a former n
with some expertise
loons, to handle techn
ters.

Stefan traced the o
Belgium, where the
and envelope were
ed. He says it is b
traditional design an
als, with two inter
naries and dual b
has good handling
and pleasant stabi
controllability. In fact
only one problem wit
ship: it leaks.

Apparently, the
rubberized-cotton f

Closeup: The Anheuser-Busch "Good Beer Blimps"

World Balloon Corporation of Albuquerque, New Mexico, has built two hot-air blimps that are leased to Anheuser-Busch for use in a promotional program for the brewer's products. World Balloon also operates the blimps under contract to the brewer. Die-hard blimp buffs might argue that these are only slightly more complicated hot-air balloons. They have propulsive power from a 180-horsepower Lycoming engine driving a ducted fan and they are fully controllable and steerable. The most significant difference between these two blimps and Goodyear's helium-filled fleet is that the former can stay aloft only so long as they have heat from their onboard propane tanks.

The engines have been converted to run on propane, too, which saves weight. The ships carry four twenty-gallon stainless-steel fuel tanks, two forward and two aft in the gondola. Fuel can be drawn from various sets of tanks to affect trim. Two standard balloon burners are installed in the roof of the gondola but angled 45 degrees forward and aft, so that their streams of hot gases are directed toward the nose and tail. By carefully controlling the flow of hot gases from each burner, fore and aft trim can be adjusted. In its initial attempt at building the airships, World Balloon found that all the hot air tended to rise and rush forward to the nose, rendering the airship almost uncontrollable. Their ingenious fix involved placing a curtain to act as a baffle between the forward and aft portions of the envelope. With the curtain in place, these "ballonets" work just fine.

In all other respects save its selection of buoyant medium, World Balloon has built two conventional airships, complete with internal catenary system and mooring lines to the envelope for the six-person ground crew. All told, it takes three to three and a half hours to unpack the blimp and ready it for flight; of that time, about twenty minutes is all that is required for inflation.

Good Beer Blimp Specifications:

Length:	175 feet
Height:	58 feet to top of tail fin
Diameter:	50 feet
Internal Volume:	229,000 feet
Weight:	2,350 pounds empty; 4,000 pounds gross weight
Materials:	3,000 yards, 2.2-ounce and four-ounce nylon
Cruise Speed:	15 to 20 knots
Capacity:	pilot + three passengers

permeable to helium and air, so that the helium is free to leak out and the air to leak in. That means that U.S. Airships can fly this airship for only a few days before it loses buoyancy and has to be reinflated with pure helium.

It has two 45-horsepower snowmobile engines that turn at 7,000 rpm with a two-to-one reduction gear to the propeller. Stefan says the tandem (fore-and-aft) gondola is well thought out, but the ballonet crossfeed controls do not work well enough; if they lose an engine, they lose the use of a ballonet. Are they discouraged? Did Columbus listen to his crew?

U.S. Airships has decided that the Australian blimp may do for an interim period, maybe performing some advertising duties but mostly serving as a training ship for their crews. That is all temporary until they can complete their next project: an all-new, 115-foot-long, twenty-eight-foot-diameter blimp. With 50,000 cubic feet of helium, the new model will lift a payload of 550 pounds and stay aloft for six hours at thirty knots. The engines and even the envelope manufacturer have not yet been selected, but Karl Stefan is not looking for any technological breakthroughs in either area. U.S. Airships just wants a plain old blimp; nothing fancy, thank you. Just so long as it is all theirs.

If you wanted to start in the blimp business, though, it would make a lot of sense to look around for other jobs that blimps of modest size can do well and *have* done well in the past. At the top of the list, you would have to place the navy's operations during World War II. Long-range, long-endurance patrols are still the single best mission that blimps ever performed. Too bad there is no job like that open today. Or is there?

The United States Coast Guard decided to study its missions to see where airships might fit in. That study was completed and the results are in: the blimp not only fits, but it fits very well into eight of the typical search, rescue, and patrol responsibilities of the Coast Guard. Goodyear is currently working on a conceptual design study for the Coast Guard under the management of the U.S. Navy's expertise at aircraft development. This is not just an idea but a funded project that is moving along briskly. Out of it would emerge a new blimp called the modern conventional airship, or MCA. That term has been selected because the MCA is as traditional in its overall configuration as it is modern in its vectored thrust and equipment. Goodyear Aerospace also has some new tools at hand that it lacked when it designed airships in World War II, and the most important of these is *computer-aided design*. Using the computer, Goodyear can design, build, and fly a conceptual airship, determine the results of the "flight" and alter any element of the new blimp to see how the change affects performance. Obviously, the computer does all this a lot more cheaply than the old method, wherein you first built a real blimp, then flew it to find out how well you had designed it. Is Goodyear serious in its pursuit of the future airship market? It is serious enough to have spent one million dollars a year for more than a decade on in-house research and engineering.

Although the new Coast Guard blimps are still far from reality, the general idea for their configuration has appeared in artists' concepts and in publications. Goodyear calls the airship the model ZP-3G. Its envelope is designed to contain 875,000 cubic feet of helium to provide a lift capacity of 55,335 pounds at sea level. Its three 800-horsepower turboprop engines would be mounted at two points well forward of the gondola and higher on the envelope than engines on past airships. The third engine would be mounted on a swiveling control surface on the stern of the airship. The front engines would be vectorable; that is, they could be swiveled to provide thrust over an arc of 180 degrees and their propellers would be reversible. The rear engine swivels upward 90 degrees and blasts air back over an inverted V-shaped control surface that turns with the engine and exerts a powerful controlling force on the tail. In cruise, the two forward engines could be shut down and the blimp operated on the stern engine alone to save fuel.

The Coast Guard program would initially make use of a modified public-relations-type blimp incorporating the vectorable propulsion system to prove its effectiveness, then a prototype for the final patrol airship. A fleet of ten airships might constitute a reasonable first order, and already, the British Royal Navy is suggesting that it might be very interested in the program if it proceeds further. At the end of 1980, a schedule of funding had been planned for this project, the first movement toward a new airship in years.

But when we talk about the future of blimps and other airships, coastal patrol and even smaller editions for possible use in police patrol over large cities are not the sort of things we will settle for. What we really like to envision is something *big,* something dazzling. The new ZP-3G Coast Guard blimp will be nice, but it will not match the ultimate airship—the hybrid vehicle—for size and spectacle.

When Goodyear printed a brochure entitled "The Rebirth of the Airship," it put a hybrid heavy-lifter on the cover. These mammoth machines use a blimp for half of their operating principle. Hybrids can match the buoyancy of airships with a winglike structure that is closer to an airplane's or they can couple a blimp envelope to a set of helicopterlike rotors. In either case, the fundamental idea behind a hybrid aircraft is to use buoyant gas to offset the empty weight of the thrust- and lift-producing machinery. A pure airplane or helicopter weighs quite a bit just parked on the ramp with the engines shut down. When you fire up the propulsion system, it must first lift the weight of the vehicle itself before it can go to work lifting a payload, and that is wasteful. Hybrids would *allow* all the horsepower from the propulsion system to be put to useful work lifting payload by using a buoyant gas to lift the engines, airframe, gondola, and whatever other machinery needed to be carried.

Both NASA and Goodyear are pursuing the hybrid heavy-lifter for the commercial market. Although eventual military use is certainly not ruled out, military airships are not a necessary step before this idea can progress. Basically, the heavy-lift airship, or HLA, has proceeded from a crude crossframe tying together four helicopters with a simple bag overhead to a more sophisticated system of rotors alone matched with conventional propellers for forward and reverse thrust and a triple-finned bag for improved pitch control in cruise.

NASA would like to build a testbed aircraft to demonstrate the flying characteristics of such a hybrid, and it has planned funds to proceed with an actual airship. A company in Philadelphia called Piasecki Aircraft and headed by helicopter designer Frank Piasecki aims to build a simple hybrid four-rotor airship out of some helicopters and a surplus blimp envelope from storage. Piasecki announced that it had been awarded a multi-million-dollar contract to demonstrate a flying airship, and although no airship had been built by the close of 1980, work was reported by Piasecki to be progressing.

Another company successfully flew a hybrid airship that was controllable like an airplane. Called the Aereon, this computer-designed aircraft was a rigid body of fairly tidy dimensions but with the interior volume of a DC-3 transport. The idea behind the Aereon was similar to that of other hybrids: use lifting gas to offset the empty weight of the lifting and propulsion machinery, so that the lift and thrust could be put to work on payload. This chubby little demonstrator, which flew without any lifting gas inside it, was dubbed "The Deltoid Pumpkin Seed" in a book of the same name by writer John McPhee. The name describes its shape better than most names do. The test pilot for the Aereon, John Olcott, is now an editor for a prominent aviation magazine. He says that aside from the normal and expected trickiness in high yaw angles that is entirely attributable to its delta shape, the Aereon flew exactly as intended and as the computer predicted—in fact, very much like an airplane.

The range of ideas and of successful demonstrations of designs for advanced airships makes it obvious that future airships are getting plenty of attention. But talking about them and even building demonstrators is relatively easy compared to the actual production of a fleet of large commercial aircraft. Morris B. Jobe, now retired from his position as chief executive officer of Goodyear Aerospace, suggested that the rebirth of airships would require an inordinately well-timed confluence of technology and design with markets and usage. And the final ingredient, of course, is money. If you check those items off one by one, you find a little of each element in place. Therefore, the closer we get to the year 2000, the more inevitable airships begin to look. To corrupt an old phrase, hang on to your airship tickets, folks—the blimp shall rise again! □

GOODYEAR
MAYFLOWER
N1A

9

50 QUESTIONS MOST OFTEN ASKED ABOUT THE BLIMP

1 How can I get a ride on the blimp?

Rides on the Goodyear blimps are available at the invitation of the company only, and they are allotted by the district manager of the area in which the blimp is operating. Most of the lucky riders are Goodyear customers, local dignitaries, or members of the press. A limited number of rides are made available for a fee to the general public, but only on the new *Enterprise* (which recently replaced its little predecessor, the *Mayflower*) and only when it is at its Florida base (near Pompano Beach). Rides are assigned on a first-call, first-served basis. The price is $7.50 for adults and $5.00 for children.

2 How many Goodyear blimps are there?

There are four: the *Enterprise,* based at Pompano Beach, Florida; the *America,* based in Spring, Texas, near Houston; the *Columbia,* based in Gardena, California, near Los Angeles; and the *Europa,* based near Rome, Italy. Goodyear has operated as many as eight blimps at a time since its first commercial airship, the *Pilgrim,* flew in 1925.

3 Are there any other airships besides Goodyear's?

There are more plans than actual airships, but the idea of carrying advertisements on airships seems to be catching on again, and there are new announcements ranging from flights of single-seat blimps —Cameron Balloons in England has flown what appears to be a barrage balloon modified to be steerable and inflated with hot air—to more conventional helium-buoyed airships. In the United States, a pair of hot-air blimps is operating to promote beer for Anheuser-Busch, and a new company in Texas called U.S. Airships recently acquired an Australian blimp to use for aerial advertising; however, the Texans may build new blimps of their own design as well. In England, an air freight company called Redcoat Cargo Airlines has ordered four 600-foot-long airships from Airship Industries, a company based on the Isle of Man. Each airship will carry a price tag of £4 million (about $9.3 million). An American air freight company, Federal Express, opened talks with Airship Industries in 1981. In late 1980, a manufacturer of fashion jeans located a used blimp, painted it gold, and planned to fly it around New York City and various public events to promote their product. For whatever reason, the blimp ran into trouble shortly after takeoff and crashed; nothing but its backers' pride was hurt.

4 Does the navy have a blimp fleet?

The United States Navy used blimps for antisubmarine patrol duty in World War II and as radar picket platforms in the 1950s, but it decommissioned the last of its lighter-than-air fleet in 1962.

5 What are the blimp's dimensions?

The Goodyear blimps measure approximately 192 feet long, 50 feet in diameter, and 59 feet high, with a volume of 202,700 cubic feet. The *Mayflower,* which was recently retired after years of service, had a smaller envelope measuring 160 feet long, 51 feet in diameter, and 58 feet high, with 147,300 cubic feet of helium capacity.

6 Is the shape of the blimp important?

Very important. The blimp's envelope is carefully designed. It is really a very large, solid airfoil called a *body of revolution,* which means that it is designed from a single curve rotated 360 degrees to form a solid that is axisymmetric, or the same no matter which way you look at it from the side and front. This large, round airfoil can create lift if it is tilted in any direction. With its nose tipped upward, it creates upward lift. Push the nose down, and the shape of the envelope will help to create a downward force—like lift, but pointed to the ground. In similar fashion, turns to the left and right involve a lift component that points to either side and allows the blimp to make the turn.

7 How much does the blimp weigh?

Without any lifting gas, the empty airship weighs about 12,000 pounds. When inflated the blimp's weight is offset by the lift of its helium.

8 What is the blimp made of?

The Goodyear blimps are fabricated by Goodyear Aerospace at the company's facility in Litchfield Park, Arizona. They are made of a special Dacron fabric coated with neoprene. They look shiny and metallic from a distance because of their reflective aluminized coating, which protects the rubber from the sun, but the envelope is actually soft and flexible.

9 Would a fire make the blimp explode?

Unlike the German zeppelins of fifty years ago, the Goodyear blimps are filled with helium, an inert gas that will not burn under any conditions. Although hydrogen is more plentiful than helium and is a slightly better lifting gas because it is lighter, it is terribly flammable, even explosive. Helium is found in the earth, mixed with other natural gases. The most significant deposits yet discovered are in northern Texas, Kansas, and Colorado.

10 Exactly what happened to the *Hindenburg*?

While the huge German zeppelin was making a landing at Lakehurst, New Jersey, on May 6, 1937, a fire started in the tail and within seconds the ship's six million cubic feet of hydrogen were ablaze. The airship was totally destroyed and thirty-six passengers and crew members were killed. The fire might have been touched off by static electricity, or it might have been the act of a saboteur. The truth will probably never be known.

11 What happens if the ship loses power in both engines?

The chance of that happening is infinitesimally small. But if it did, the pilot could fly the ship as he would a free balloon—one without engines and controls—gradually valving off helium to allow the blimp to descend. If just one engine should fail, the blimp could easily fly and maintain ballonet pressure by using the other engine.

12 What happens if the blimp gets a hole in it?

The gas in the blimp is at very low pressure, so the ship could sustain a surprisingly large tear and still maintain its shape long enough to land. But since there is no internal structure inside the envelope, the gas would eventually escape and the blimp would become as flat as any other deflated balloon.

13 Why is the *America* sometimes referred to as the "ghost blimp"?

Early in World War II, the navy blimp L-8 left Moffett Field in California on a routine antisubmarine patrol flight over the Pacific. Two naval officers, Lieutenant Cody and Ensign Adams, were aboard. When the L-8 had been out for about an hour, Cody radioed that they had spotted an oil slick and were investigating. Then, nothing. That message was the last ever heard from the two men. Later the same day, the blimp was spotted nudged against a cliff on a beach south of San Francisco. As rescuers approached, the ship dislodged itself and drifted inland. It floated down in Daly City, made a perfect landing on its single wheel, and came to a stop at an intersection.

No one was aboard the L-8, and no one has ever been able to account for the disappearance of Cody and Adams. The throttles were at idle, everything was working normally, there was fuel in the tanks, and the cabin door was open. Some local volunteer firemen slashed the envelope, completely destroying it, in the mistaken belief that the crew might be trapped inside. Only the car was saved.

This car, designated C-64, was refurbished after the war and is now in service on the Houston-based *America*.

14 How is helium made?

Aside from a thermonuclear reaction, helium cannot be made, nor can it be destroyed. Helium is an inert gas, which means that it will not combine chemically with anything. It is found only in nature, concentrated for the most part in natural gas deposits found in a few areas of the United States. Since it will not burn, companies that sell natural gas need to separate the helium from the combustible gases. They do this by using separation processing that divides each type of gas found in the mixture on the basis of its physical properties. Helium is, in that sense, a by-product of the separation process.

15 How often does the helium have to be added?

The airships lose very little helium in normal operation, although the gas does have to be purified by a purifying machine about once a year. As the envelopes age and become slightly porous, the crew might have to add as much as 10,000 cubic feet of gas per month. They buy the gas on the road and add it as it is needed, since none is carried along.

16 If the airship does not release helium, how does it come down?

Inside the envelope are two air chambers called *ballonets*, one forward and one aft. They can be pumped up with air from the outside or allowed to deflate as the helium expands when the blimp climbs into thinner air. Since air is heavier than helium, inflating or deflating the ballonets will add or subtract weight from the nose or tail, thereby trimming the airship. Using the ballonets, the airship can sail up or down within the ocean of air and maintain its proper envelope pressure without having to drop ballast or valve off helium. The two hanging scoops behind the propellers are air intakes for the ballonets; the props force air into them when the pilot opens them up. When the airship is on the ground and the engines shut down, special auxiliary electric blowers automatically maintain the proper pressure in the ballonets.

17 Could the airship somehow get loose from its mast and float away?

The hitching mechanism is designed to anchor the blimp in extremely strong winds, and failure is very unlikely. Should the airship somehow break its mooring, a zipperlike panel at the top of the envelope, which is tied to the mast by a long rope, would tear the envelope open as the blimp moved away. The opening would vent the helium and deflate the hapless blimp before it could fly very far. The automatic rip-panel is a necessary safety feature on all blimps.

18 How is the airship anchored when it is on the ground?

At the very tip of the blimp's nose is a steel ball much like an automobile's trailer hitch. This ball locks onto a cup at the top of the portable mooring mast, which is taken along and set up wherever the blimp is operating. The blimp is anchored to the earth only at this one point, so it is always free to rotate 360 degrees around the mast as the wind changes. This arrangement has held the blimp in hurricane-force winds on more than one occasion. The blimp will always point itself into the wind, like a weather vane.

19 What are those two ropes at the nose?

The nose lines are used to hold the airship's nose into the wind while it is being handled on the ground. The blimp has so much "sail area" that it would become dangerously unmanageable if it were somehow to move sideways to the wind. Therefore, two groups of three ground-crew members grab each line as the airship lands, then run off to both sides and hold the nose steady at the direction of the crew chief. The two lines are allowed to hang down and trail in the air when the airship is flying, since there is no particular reason to pull them in or tie them off.

20 What are those little round bags for?

They are ballast bags, each filled with twenty-five pounds of lead shot. They are put into or taken out of a little compartment at the rear of the car to give a final trim before liftoff and help compensate for loss of fuel weight as the blimp operates through the day. The ballast bags are used by the crew chief to trim the weight prior to takeoff. The crew chief and pilot calculate the weight of fuel and payload (including passengers), then add or subtract shot bags as desired. Pilots usually like to take off about "four bags down," or 100 pounds heavy.

21 Why does the crew chief hold up that "butterfly net" when the blimp lands?

That is a little portable wind sock, and it gives the pilot a final check on the wind direction as he makes his approach. The airship must land directly into the wind. If there is a last-minute wind shift, the pilot will see it in the sock. He will then push the throttles to full power and make another try after a go-around.

22 Can blimps land anywhere they want to?

Because they land at very low airspeeds and can virtually stop in midair as soon as they near the ground, a blimp can theoretically land almost anywhere. The United States Navy has operated them from large airfields and from tiny aircraft carriers. The most important practical consideration is not the landing itself but the mooring. For that reason a landing site must be accessible to the ground crew and allow enough room for the moored blimp to swing with changes in the wind. It helps if the landing site is fairly clear of obstructions, too, so that the wind is less turbulent and the chances of striking a building or a phone pole are reduced. That is why Goodyear's blimp crews stick mostly to airports or very large, open fields.

23 What happens to the blimp in the rain?

First of all, it gets wet. What

matters is that there is so much of the blimp to get wet! The surface area of the envelope is so big that all those raindrops add up to a lot of water—and a lot of weight. Depending upon how much rain is coming down, the water might add hundreds of pounds to the basic airframe weight. Rain also tends to cool the blimp if it has been heated by the sun, and the sum of both effects —cooling and added weight— makes it less buoyant.

24 Since the blimp floats, what is that tire under the car used for?

The blimp's single-wheel landing gear under the gondola supports it as it slowly rises and falls on its mooring. The blimp may float, but it still needs something to fend off contact with the earth. The gear also swivels freely to allow the blimp to swing in the wind. When the blimp is heavy, such as it might be before a long television flight, it uses a short rolling takeoff similar to an airplane's, and that is when it needs its landing wheel most.

25 How many lights are there on the sides of the airship?

There are 7,560 on each of the four GZ-20 airships. The smaller GZ-19 *Mayflower* mounted 3,080 when it was in operation. The lights are actually auto taillight bulbs, covered with red, yellow, blue, and green discs.

26 Does Goodyear build its own blimps?

Yes, indeed. The envelopes and other components are fabricated by Goodyear Aerospace, and final erection takes place at the airship hangar in Houston. It takes twenty-five workers six weeks to put everything together. Each ship has to be rebuilt with a new envelope every six years or so. The gondolas, however, are just refurbished and put back in the air. Most of them date back to World War II and some even earlier.

27 How does the night sign work?

Goodyear calls it the Super Skytacular, and they keep the details of its operation under their hats. Basically, it is a complicated electronic system that reads impulses on a magnetic tape and sends out thousands of commands to turn the right lights on and off at the proper instant. The tapes are programmed by computer at the Goodyear Aerospace Night Sign Laboratory in Akron. They can design messages that will say or do practically anything.

28 What kinds of engines do the blimps have?

There are two engines on each blimp, both of them Continental IO-360s, fuel-injected, direct-drive, and rated at 210-horsepower each. These are the same engines as those used to propel the Cessna Skymaster. The propellers are Hartzell pushers, constant speed and reversible. They are custom-made for the Goodyear blimps.

The old *Mayflower* used some rare engines that are no longer in production: the 175-horsepower Continental GO-300s, which are carbureted and geared down to produce a propeller speed slower than the crankshaft speed. They used to power the Cessna 175 Skylark.

The blimps also carry special auxiliary power units to generate electricity for the many lights of the night signs. These special turbine generators are made by Garrett AiResearch, and they are similar to the units that provide ground power to airliners.

29 How fast and how far can the blimp go?

The usual cruising speed is thirty-five miles per hour; all-out top speed is fifty-three miles per hour. That is if there is no wind. Any head- or tailwind can be added or subtracted to get the airship's speed over the ground. When the wind gets much above twenty knots (about twenty-three miles per hour), the airship is usually put on the mast until the weather calms down a bit. Wind will not actually hurt the blimp when it is flying, but the airship becomes very hard to handle near the ground.

About cruising range: the airship could carry enough fuel to fly for twenty-four hours if it had to, although it rarely does. When traveling cross-country (remember that blimps fly wherever they go, regardless of the distance) the crews try for an eight-hour day, or about 300 air miles.

30 What kinds of radios and instruments do the blimps use?

All Goodyear blimps are certified by the Federal Aviation Administration for flight in instrument meteorological conditions under IFR (Instrument Flight Rules) either day or night. They carry two navigation and communication transceivers, the usual instruments found in any airplane, digital radar for keeping an eye on thunderstorms, a transponder for radar identification with air traffic controllers, and a couple of instruments peculiar to blimps: manometers for watching envelope pressure and a helium temperature gauge. Blimps are also equipped with navigation systems that can provide landing guidance in instrument conditions, including a glide slope and localizer receiver. As aerial navigation is a bit more complex in the airspace system of Europe, the *Europa* also carries an ADF (Automatic Direction Finder) and two DME (Distance Measuring Equipment) systems. The *Europa* also carries, in addition to its flight equipment, a fancy little cassette tape machine that announces to admiring onlookers pertinent facts about the airship in any of ten languages.

31 Is there a kitchen or a bathroom aboard?

No and no. The pilots usually take along a picnic lunch on cross-country flights, the junior man taking care of the grocery shopping. There is a relief tube for the men, but the women are in for a tough time on long trips.

32 What is the blimp worth? Are they for sale?

Since Goodyear builds them one at a time, it is very difficult to put a price tag on a Goodyear blimp. The company says that if it started from scratch to build one in 1980, it would cost about $5 million. Goodyear currently builds blimps only for use by its own public relations department.

33 How many crewmen and pilots are there for each airship?

The usual complement is seventeen crewmen (riggers, engine mechanics, ground handlers, and electronic technicians), five pilots, and a public relations representative. Crew members share driving chores in the bus and truck, and they take turns standing watch over the airship whenever it is moored. The blimps are never, *never* left alone.

34 How do the pilots learn to fly blimps?

Since the pool of qualified airship drivers is limited, to say the least, Goodyear has little choice but to train its own pilots. All Goodyear LTA pilots are also certified as instructors, and they share teaching duties when a new pilot is assigned to any of the operations. Openings do not come up very often, and there are always hundreds of applications on file. Goodyear takes applications only from fixed-wing pilots who already have commercial, instrument, and multi-engine ratings. A college education is also a big bonus for an applicant.

35 How do the other crewmen get their jobs?

Again, experienced blimp crews are hard to find, except in the case of mechanics, since blimps use regular lightplane engines. Many of the permanent crewmen originally worked as part-time "field wage" hands during the winter off-season. The jobs seem great, and they really are a lot of fun, but they are not for everyone. The blimps spend between six and eight months a year on the road, and that can quickly turn into a monotonous blur of motel rooms for anyone who does not truly love to travel. Many of the crew members have families who accompany them on their summer tours.

36 What does it cost Goodyear to operate a blimp for one year?

The annual budget is now about $1.6 million per year per ship, including payroll, equipment, depreciation, travel expenses, and maintenance. In Europe, where everything from fuel to hotel rooms is more expensive, the cost is double that figure.

37 What does Goodyear get in return for such a huge outlay?

The end result is corporate-name recognition and good will. Independent research has demonstrated that people are excited by seeing the blimp and are able to remember when and where they saw it. Over sixty million Americans get a first-hand look at the three United States blimps every year, and more viewers see them on television. The Goodyear blimps may therefore be the best-known corporate symbol in America.

38 Is there a future for big airships?

The great zeppelins of the 1920s and 1930s were ahead of their time, and many people feel that with advances in materials, weather forecasting, and computer technology, large airships could be built today with far greater performance, strength, and reliability. Large airships could indeed serve as short-haul, heavy-lift cargo carriers, and their operational efficiency might prove to be very impressive, particularly in remote locations far from roads and rivers.

However, the capital outlay that would be required for research, development, and prototype construction of an all-new airship technology would run into the hundreds of millions of dollars and at the present time only governments are that wealthy. It is a subject about which some people become very emotional and unrealistic. It would indeed be grand to see the huge passenger-carrying airships fly again, but the hard numbers stand in the way. However, very large utility blimps that carry heavy, bulky cargo for short distances might be profitable in the future.

39 Will Goodyear build big airships again?

Goodyear has no definite plans in the immediate future to expand its airship operations into larger airships. A serious effort by government or industry to renew interest in airships could possibly change all that, however.

40 How big were the zeppelins compared to the Goodyear blimps?

The *Hindenburg* was the largest, and it was 804 feet long, more than four times the length of the larger Goodyear GZ-20s. Its gas volume was over six million cubic feet, and it had 242 tons of gross lift —enough to carry itself plus seventy passengers, a crew of sixty, diesel fuel for a transatlantic flight, luggage, some cargo and mail, and twenty tons of water ballast that could be dropped in the event of an emergency. It was much faster, too, cruising at up to eighty miles per hour.

41 What is it like to ride in a Goodyear blimp?

It is the flight of dreams—smooth, slow, and close to the ground. The cabin windows can be opened on a nice day, and passengers (the airship carries only six) can lean out and wave to people on the ground. You can see the ground in far greater detail than from a plane, and a given point stays in view for much longer, since the airship moves at only thirty-five miles per hour.

42 What is it like to fly the blimp?

The blimp has a life of its own in the air. Its movements are slow and ponderous, and yet it reacts very intimately to air currents and thermals. It takes several long seconds for the airship to respond to the pilot's commands, and, as a result, good pilots soon develop a sixth sense that helps them to counteract the blimp's wanderings.

The control surfaces are as big as barn doors, and they are not power-assisted. On a turbulent day, the pilot might find himself jamming both feet onto one big rudder pedal in order to force the ship into a turn. For the most part, however, the blimp is a joy to fly. The slow cruise speed is a special treat for a pilot who is used to fixed-wing flight, since he or she can gaze out and observe the passing landscape in much finer detail.

43 Is the blimp quiet?

Hot-air balloons that float with the breeze are truly quiet (except when their burners are operating), but the blimp has two airplane engines with propellers only a few feet away from the cabin window so there is a good deal of noise, particularly on takeoff. The sound level is not unpleasant, however, and once level at cruise, passengers almost completely forget about the noise.

44 Do people get airsick in the blimp?

It is less likely than in almost any other aircraft. On a long flight on a turbulent day it is possible to get seasick, since the blimp will pitch and roll like a seagoing vessel. Fortunately, the envelope is flexible and absorbs the bumps on normal flights, and the ride is usually as smooth as can be.

45 How high does the blimp usually fly?

Most flights, whether with passengers or cross-country, are at 1,000 to 1,500 feet above the ground, but not more. Goodyear likes to keep the airship close to the ground so that people can see it more easily. It has a maximum altitude, depending upon variations in atmospheric conditions, of about 5,000 feet. Beyond that height the air gets thinner and the helium expands too much, causing automatic safety valves to open.

47 Is the blimp safe?

Goodyear has flown passengers in its blimps for more than forty years without interruption (except during World War II), and no passenger has ever so much as scratched a finger. It is probably the safest form of air travel ever devised.

46 Could an airship ever get stuck up there?

That was a serious consideration for some of the long-range dirigibles that arrived at a destination with a severe *inversion layer* and with a light ship due to fuel burn-off. (An inversion layer is a weather condition wherein the air a few hundred feet above the surface is actually warmer than the air below, the opposite of normal conditions wherein the air cools at higher altitudes; hence the term *inversion.*) A blimp flying in warm air will soak up some heat in its own helium, thereby becoming even lighter when it tries to descend into denser, cooler air below. Even with the nose pointed down and at high engine power, the airship may be too light to descend. Zeppelins arriving at Los Angeles were reported to have gotten stuck aloft, and they had to circle until evening, when their hydrogen cooled enough to allow a descent.

48 How does the television camera in the blimp work?

Goodyear has its own specially designed television equipment for use in the blimps. The equipment is kept in Akron and shipped by air for installation just prior to a given event. The camera is a small color unit mounted in a vibration-free gimbal. The lens is an enormous 30:1 zoom. The camera's image is transmitted to the ground by microwave, where a dish antenna and receiver pick it up and feed it to the network. The blimp's signal can be put on the air live or taped for replay. Goodyear pilots fly the blimp and the company supplies the equipment free of charge to the networks, as it has done for years.

49 What events do the blimps cover for television?

It varies from year to year, but the list is impressive. To date, they have given audiences air views of the Indianapolis 500 automobile race, the Kentucky Derby, the Super Bowl, the World Series, the Rose Bowl and Parade, the America's Cup yacht races, the U.S. Tennis Open at Forest Hills and Flushing Meadow, and the magnificent Bicentennial Tall Ships parade up the Hudson River near New York City.

50 How can we get the blimp to come to our county fair or pea-picking contest?

Each year, the blimps receive thousands of requests for their presence. The complexity of moving the ship slowly around the country means that only a few of the requests can be honored. Nevertheless, the ships are on the road every year, and Goodyear is always interested in new events to visit. The Public Relations Department, Goodyear Tire & Rubber Company, Akron, Ohio 44316, will be glad to hear your request.

INDEX